NUT**SHELLS**

Constitutional and Administrative Law

NUT**SHELLS**

Constitutional and Administrative Law

NINTH EDITION

by
RICHARD GLANCEY,
EIMEAR SPAIN AND
RHONA SMITH

SWEET & MAXWELL

THOMSON REUTERS

First Edition – 1987
Second Edition – 1990
Third Edition – 1993
Fourth Edition – 1996
Fifth Edition – 1998
Sixth Edition – 2002
Seventh Edition – 2005
Eighth Edition – 2008

Published in 2011 by Sweet & Maxwell, 100 Avenue Road, London, NW3 3PF
part of Thomson Reuters (Professional) UK Limited
(Registered in England & Wales, Company No 1679046.
Registered Office and address for service:
Aldgate House, 33 Aldgate High Street, London EC3N 1DL)

*For further information on our products and services, visit
www.sweetandmaxwell.co.uk

Typeset by YHT Ltd
Printed in Great Britain by Ashford Colour Press, Gosport, Hants

No natural forests were destroyed to make this product;
only farmed timber was used and re-planted

A CIP catalogue record for this book is available from the British Library.

ISBN: 978-0-41404-594-1

Thomson Reuters and the Thomson Reuters logo are trademarks of Thomson Reuters.
Sweet & Maxwell ® is a registered trademark of Thomson Reuters (Professional) UK Limited.

Crown copyright material is reproduced with the permission of the Controller
of HMSO and the Queen's Printer for Scotland.

Contents

Using this Book

Welcome to our new look NUTSHELLS revision series. We have revamped and improved the existing design and layout and added new features, according to student feedback.

NEW DETAILED TABLE OF CONTENTS for easy navigation.

REDESIGNED TABLES OF CASES AND LEGISLATION for easy reference.

NEW CHAPTER INTRODUCTIONS to outline
the key concepts covered and condense
complex and important information.

Other Statutory R.

NATIONAL MINIMUM WAGE ACT

The National Minimum Wage Act 19
minimum hourly rate of pay for all v
tate to determine and amer
are set: one

**DEFINITION CHECKPOINTS AND
EXPLANATION OF KEY CASES**
to highlight important information.

ine HL reversed the
not customary and did need t.

> **DEFINITION CHECKPOINT**
> Procession
> The **Public Order Act 1986**, s.16 de.
> sion in a public place. This is not ov
> nition can be found in the case of *Flo*
> at 502, where Lord Goddard C.J. sta
> *body of persons: it is a body, of pe*

> **DEFINITION CHECKPOINT**
> Assembly
> The **Public Order Act 1986**
> mbly of two or r

> **KEY CASE**
>
> CARMICHAEL V NATIONAL POW.
> Mrs Carmichael worked as a gu
> required" basis, showing group:
> tion. She worked some hours m(
> wore a company uniform, was s
> vehicle, and enjoyed many of th
> question for the court to determ'
> "umbrella" or "global" emplov
> which she worked and the i⌐
>
> **Held:** (HL) During tho·
> ꞈng her duti·

DIAGRAMS, FLOWCHARTS AND OTHER DIAGRAMMATIC REPRESENTATION to clarify and condense complex and important information and break up the text.

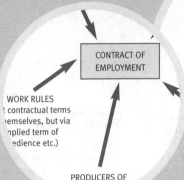

Figure 1 Court and Tribunal System

House of Lords

COURT OF APPEAL (CIVIL DIVISION)

EMPLOYMENT APPEAL TRIBUNAL

CONTRACT OF EMPLOYMENT

WORK RULES
t contractual terms
emselves, but via
nplied term of
edience etc.)

PRODUCERS OF COLLECTIVE

END OF CHAPTER REVISION CHECKLISTS outlining what you should now know and understand.

Chapter Checklist

You should now know and unders

- the three heads of claim for
- issues regarding the choice of
- the role of the independent e:
- what is meant by "pay".

QUESTION AND AN

END OF CHAPTER QUESTION AND ANSWER SECTION with advice on relating knowledge to examination performance, how to approach the question, how to structure the answer, the pitfalls (and how to avoid them!) and how to get the best marks.

QUESTION AND ANSWER

The Question

David and Emily are employed as machi
worked for them for one and a half yea

Emily discovers that David earns £9.0
paid £8.50 per hour. She also disc
employed by a subsidiary of XCo ir

HANDY HINTS AND USEFUL WEBSITES
– revision and examination tips and
advice relating to the subject features
at the end of the book, along with a list of useful websites.

HANDY HINTS

Examination questions in employme
either essay questions or problem ques
format and in what is required of the ex
of question in turn.

Students usually prefer one type
normally opting for the problem ques
examinations are usually set in a way
least one of each style of question

Very few, if any, questions
ows about a topic, and it
make a p

USEFUL WEBSITES

Official Information
www.parliament.uk—very user-friendly.
www.direct.gov.uk—portal for governme
www.opsi.gov.uk—Office of Public Secto
   and statutory instruments available
www.dca.gov.uk—Department for Con
www.dca.gov.uk/peoples-rights/hum
   Unit at the Department for Con
www.homeoffice.gov.uk/police/
the **Police and Criminal**

NEW COLOUR CODING throughout to
help distinguish cases and legislation
from the narrative. At the first mention,
cases are highlighted in colour and
italicised and legislation is highlighted
in colour and emboldened.

aw has d
are an ethnic group (*Seic*
ypsies are an ethnic group (*CRE*
Rastafarians are not an ethnic group
ment [1993] I.R.L.R. 284)
(d) Jehovah's Witnesses are not an ethnic o
   Norwich City College case 1502237/97)
(e) RRA covers the Welsh (*Gwynedd CC v Jone*
(f) Both the Scots and the English are covere
   "national origins" but not by "ethnic or
   Board v Power [1997], *Boyce v British Ai*

It should be noted that Sikhs, Jews, Je
ians are also protected on
Equality (Religion or P

Table of Cases

Table of Statutes

Introduction

"Constitutional and Administrative" or "Public" Law

"Constitutional and Administrative Law" is a core subject for a qualifying law degree. It is sometimes taught under the title of "Public Law". It is a very broad subject area covering a wide range of topics. The topics included in the study of Public Law will vary across different institutions. The topics included in this Nutshells book cover the most popular topics and are thus taught by most institutions. This book should therefore serve as a useful guide to the topic regardless of where the subject is studied.

At the heart of Constitutional and Administrative Law is the study of laws that impact upon citizens, the state and their relationship between each other. Within this broad remit, topics such as Constitutional Law, Police Powers and Judicial Review are all included. What these very different topics all have in common is their impact upon the relationship between the individual and the state in one form or another.

The "Constitutional" law topics included in this book are: The Nature of the UK Constitution; The Executive; Parliament; The Police and the Public; and Protest and Public Order. The "Administrative" law topics in this book are the final two chapters on Judicial Review and Remedies.

When studying Constitutional and Administrative Law, it is important to keep up-to-date with political developments. While the majority of the topic does look at "Law", an awareness of the political arena is also needed to fully understand the area. The main "people" within Constitutional Law, such as the Government and the Houses of Parliament, are political organs, so keeping up to date with political developments is recommended.

To help illustrate this point, many rules that govern Constitutional Law were seen in practice in the summer of 2010 when the Labour Government lost its majority in the House of Commons and the coalition Government between the Conservatives and the Liberal Democrats took power. Because there was a "hung Parliament" (nobody won an overall majority in the Commons) Gordon Brown, as the current Prime Minister at the time, remained in office and was given the first opportunity to try and form an alliance with another party in order to obtain a majority of Commons' seats, even though he did not win the election. This is a constitutional "rule" and is known as a "Constitutional Convention". Constitutional Conventions are a source of the UK constitution and are discussed in Ch.2. This is just one example of Constitutional Law in practice and the inter-relationship between law and politics. Keeping an eye on news stories and applying the law to them helps to bring a deeper level of understanding to the area and makes the law "real". This book was accurate on submission in September 2010, and where possible, has been updated at proof stage.

Constitutional and Administrative law contains a wonderful mix of black letter law and the study of theory. Black letter law is studied within the topic of Police Powers and Public Order, whilst when studying the topic of the Nature of the UK Constitution recourse to different theories is needed—such as theories about the Rule of Law and Parliamentary Supremacy. Rather than being "put off" by theory, take this opportunity to enjoy studying Public Law as it is a fantastic way to explore the theories for yourself and enables you to form your own opinion about the fundamental nature of the legal system into which you may want to forge your career.

Finally, whilst the current authors have thoroughly updated and revised this book, they have tried to remain true to the content selected by Greer Hogan, who authored the first eight very successful editions. Greer is now enjoying her retirement.

The Nature of the UK Constitution

. . . .

INTRODUCTION

Most countries have a written document known as "the constitution" which lays down the main rules governing the structure and functions of government, which regulates the relationship between the state and its citizens and provides a measure of the legitimacy of government actions. Typically such constitutions are to some degree entrenched, that is, the constitutional rules are more difficult to change than ordinary laws, perhaps requiring approval by referendum (Republic of Ireland) or special majority (United States). Such constitutions also tend to have a higher status than ordinary laws thus creating the need for a high level judicial body with the power to declare laws passed in contravention of the constitution invalid.

The position is not so straightforward in the UK, a country with one of the oldest parliaments in the world. There is no single document containing the constitution, rather a selection of different sources are drawn on. To understand the UK's constitution, you must understand:

- the nature and scope of the constitution;
- sources of the UK constitution, including statutes, cases and conventions;
- the doctrine of supremacy of Parliament;
- the rule of law.

. . . .

CHARACTERISTICS OF THE BRITISH CONSTITUTION

DEFINITION CHECKPOINT

In Public Law, a constitution is the set of rules which prescribe the structure and functions of government of a specified territory. These rules are often written down in a single document and difficult or impossible to alter.

Unwritten

The UK does not have a written constitution in the sense of a formal document but that does not mean that it lacks constitutional rules. These are expressed with differing degrees of formality in the form of statutory provisions, case law and conventions of the constitution.

There are, compared to many countries, few positive statements regarding the powers and duties of the organs of government. These are simply recognised by common law and convention and are subject to various legal and conventional limitations. Our constitution historically did not contain any positive declaration of the rights of individuals in the form of a Bill of Rights. Those rules relating to such matters as freedom of speech and assembly were traditionally derived from, and had the same status as, any other legal rule. Today, the Human Rights Act 1998 (HRA) gives "further effect" to the European Convention on Human Rights (ECHR) in national law and gives rights to individuals which can be directly enforced in the UK courts.

Flexible

The British Constitution can be described as flexible in that:

(a) It does not have the rigidity of most written constitutions as Parliament can repeal any law by a simple majority. The orthodox viewpoint is that, as each successive Parliament has the power to pass or repeal any legislation, any attempt to bind Parliament by entrenching a statutory provision would be ineffective (*Ellen Street Estates Ltd v Minister of Health* (CA, 1936)). It has, however, been argued that certain fundamental Acts of Parliament such as the Act of Union with Scotland 1707 and the European Communities Act 1972 could not be repealed as, in each case, Parliament which enacted the provision is no longer in existence in the same form but has reconstituted itself as a less powerful body. In *Thoburn v Sunderland City Council* (DC, 2001), Laws L.J. expressed the view that within our law there was a hierarchy of Acts of Parliament, ordinary statutes and constitutional statutes, and that while the former may be impliedly repealed, the latter, such as the European Communities Act, could only be repealed expressly.

In any event, while in legal theory there may be complete flexibility, the political reality may be quite different. The Statute of Westminster 1931 and the various Independence Acts may, in theory, be capable of repeal, but, in practice, they are entrenched in our constitution: "Freedom once given cannot be taken away. Legal theory must give way to practical politics" (per *Lord Denning in Blackburn v The Att-Gen* (CA, 1971)).

Some writers have also argued that there are inherent limitations on what Parliament can or cannot do and that it does not have the power to pass laws contrary to fundamental human values. If, for example, it legislated to provide that "all blue eyed babies should be murdered" (Leslie Stephen, *The Science of Ethics*, 1882, p.137, also quoted in Dicey) then Lord Woolf has argued that the courts would simply refuse to uphold the law (*Droit Public—English Style*, 1995, Public Law 57).

(b) The absence of a written constitution has allowed quite considerable changes to be made informally, without amendment of these legal rules which do exist. For example, the gradual transfer of power from the House of Commons to the Cabinet occurred without any formal legislative change. Conventions, an important source of constitutional law, can be extremely flexible, reflecting changes in the political situation as and when they occur. Thus the constitution can evolve gradually.

Unitary

Because all legislative power stems from Parliament, the UK has a unitary as opposed to a federal constitution. It is certainly possible for Parliament to give limited powers of government to local authorities and to local and national assemblies but the doctrine of parliamentary sovereignty means that a subsequent Parliament can repeal the relevant legislation and take back the power. For example, this happened in 1972 when the Westminster Parliament re-imposed direct rule in Northern Ireland and in 2000 when the Northern Ireland Assembly, established under the Northern Ireland Act 1998, was suspended. Devolution of power was restored in May 2007.

. . . .

SOURCES OF THE CONSTITUTION

Legislation

Although the UK does not have a written constitution there are many Acts of Parliament relevant to constitutional law. Some fundamental steps in the constitutional development of the country (pre Treaty of Union) were the Bill of Rights 1689 which limited the power of the monarch to rule by virtue of the royal prerogative, the Act of Settlement 1700 which further strengthened the power of Parliament and provided for the succession to the English throne, and more recently, the European Communities Act 1972 which facilitated the UK's accession to the now European Union (EU) and the Human Rights Act (HRA). The actual composition of Parliament has been altered by the House of Lords Act 1999 and its powers by the Parliament Acts 1911 and 1949 (see Ch.4).

Figure 2.1: Sources of the Constitution

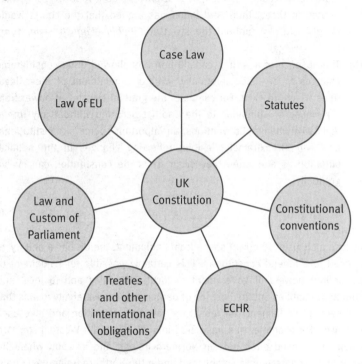

Case law

According to Dicey, writing in the nineteenth century, the British Constitution was "judge made". Even today there are many areas of constitutional law regulated not by statute but by the common law as expounded by our judges. Examples of this can be seen in the development of the doctrine of the supremacy of Parliament and, in judicial review, the establishment of a right to a fair hearing.

In recent years there has been an increased reliance on statute law, for example, in relation to public order and the powers of the police, but, of course, here too, the judges have a role to play in the interpretation of the statutory provisions (see below Chs 5 and 6).

Conventions of the Constitution

If one tries to understand the British Constitution simply by reference to case law and statute, one obtains a totally false impression. Take one example, the role played by the monarch. The Queen must give the Royal Assent to all legislation. She appoints the Prime Minister and has the power to dissolve Parliament. This might lead one to believe that the monarch still exercises considerable political power. Yet in practice we now have a constitutional monarchy where the Queen acts on the advice of her Prime Minister. The Royal Assent has not been refused since 1708 and, as the protracted negotiations between David Cameron, Nick Clegg and Gordon Brown following the general election of May 2010 aptly demonstrated, the Queen has little choice of Prime Minister. In that instance, the Queen waited for negotiations to conclude and the parties themselves to agree on who would be proposed to the Queen as the person to be invited to be Prime Minister (obviously it was David Cameron in a formal coalition with the Liberal Democrats including Nick Clegg as Deputy Prime Minister).

Such changes in the power of the monarch have arisen, not through statute, but as a result of the convention that the monarch should not become politically involved and should not be seen to favour any one political party.

This example illustrates the fact that the formal rules have to be understood against a background of constitutional conventions which can both expand and modify the strict legal rules. And so conventions have been described as "the flesh which clothes the dry bones of the law" (Ivor Jennings, *The Law and the Constitution*, 1959 p.81*)*.

What are conventions?

DEFINITION CHECKPOINT
Constitutional conventions are non-legal rules of constitutional behaviour which are considered to be binding upon those who operate the constitution but which are not enforced by the courts or by the presiding officers in Parliament.

Conventions may be recognised by the courts as part of the constitutional background against which a particular decision is taken (*Carltona v Commissioners of Works* (CA, 1943)), but will not be enforced directly. (See also *Reference Re Amendment of the Constitution of Canada* (Supreme Court of Canada, 1982)).

Conventions are not written down in any formal sense in that they are not expressed as Acts of Parliament nor are they established by judicial precedent. Occasionally an existing convention is formalised as, for example, s.43 of the **Statute of Westminster 1931**.

Important constitutional institutions such as the Cabinet and the office of Prime Minister have been created by convention. The first statutory reference to the Prime Minister came in the **Chequers Estate Act 1917**. The relationship between government and Parliament can only be understood against the background of the convention of ministerial responsibility.

Conventions thus have a central role in the development of the British Constitution.

Advantages and disadvantages of conventions
While the use of conventions can add flexibility to our constitutional rules and avoid the constant need for formal change to ensure the constitution properly reflects the realities of political life, it does provide the government with easy opportunities to amend the rules in its favour.

Other sources

The law of the European Union
By virtue of our membership of the European Union and the provisions of the European Communities Act 1972, community law is part of UK laws. The primary sources of EU law are the treaties which establish the Union. The secondary sources are regulations, directives and decisions of the Council, Parliament and the Commission as well as the jurisprudence of the European Courts of Justice.

ECHR law
An increasingly important source of public law is the European Convention for the Protection of Human Rights and Fundamental Freedoms (ECHR).

Although the UK ratified the Convention in 1951, it was not directly enforceable in our courts and individuals had to apply to the ECHR to assert their fundamental rights (see for example, *Findlay v UK* (1997) on the fairness of courts martial proceedings). This was an expensive, time consuming process as well as not in the spirit of the Convention which requires States themselves to provide adequate remedies under national laws (art.13).

The **Human Rights Act** (HRA) does not attempt to incorporate the ECHR into English law directly but it gives "further effect" to the Convention in a number of ways.

LEGISLATION HIGHLIGHTER

Human Rights Act—key provisions

Section 2: requires UK courts to take into account decisions of the ECHR.

Section 3: a new rule of statutory interpretation in s.3(1) provides that, in so far as it is possible to do so, legislation must be given effect to in a way which is compatible with Convention rights.

Section 4: the superior courts have the power to issue declarations of incompatibility where they are unable to reconcile UK law with the Convention (under s.3).

Section 19: the Government is required to indicate by Second Reading stage whether a provision is convention compliant.

Section 6: it is unlawful for public bodies to act in a way which is incompatible with Convention rights unless there is legislation to the contrary (s.6(2)).

While the term "public body" (s.6) includes courts, government bodies, local authorities and the police, it explicitly excludes Parliament itself. However, the inclusion of courts in the definition means that the Act has both horizontal and vertical effect.

Section 1 of the Act defines convention rights as arts 2–12 and 14 and arts 1–3 of the First Protocol as read with arts 16 and 18 of the Convention. Some articles such as art.3 give absolute rights. Others such as arts 8, 9, 10 and 11 are qualified rights.

The law and custom of Parliament

Parliament has the right to regulate its own procedure and does so by means of standing orders. These, together with resolutions passed by either House and the rulings given by the Speaker, are contained in *Erskine May Parliamentary Practice* (William Mckay, 23rd edn, 2004).

Treaties, conventions and other international obligations

These are not a direct source of constitutional law in the sense that they do not normally involve any change in domestic law (see however, *The Parlement Belge* (HC, 1879)). A treaty may bind the government in international law but will normally be given effect within this country by the passing of legislation. This happened in the case of membership of the EU where the signing of the various treaties was followed by the passing of the **European Communities Act 1972**. The ECHR, although ratified by Great Britain in 1951, did not, until the passage of the **HRA** in 1998, give directly enforceable rights to individuals in this country (see *R. v Home Secretary, Ex p. Brind* (HL, 1991)). UN treaties on human rights remain outwith national laws. The courts will, however, have some regard for conventions presuming that Parliament intends to comply with its international obligations (e.g. *R. v Sec of State for Education and Employment and others, Ex p. Williamson* (HL, 2005) per Baroness Hale).

Figure 2.2: Relationship between UK laws and treaties

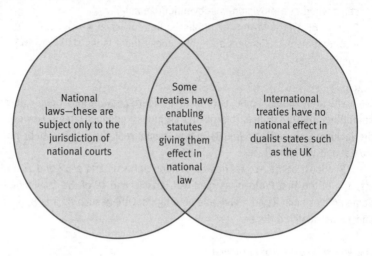

National laws—these are subject only to the jurisdiction of national courts

Some treaties have enabling statutes giving them effect in national law

International treaties have no national effect in dualist states such as the UK

THE RULE OF LAW

When we talk about the "rule of law" we are not describing a legal rule which can be enforced in court. Rather it is a principle embodied in democratic societies that power must be exercised in accordance with the law and that the law should demonstrate certain characteristics. The nature of these characteristics is, however, impossible to state with any precision. Such ideas have long been part of our legal traditions and have been considered of particuar significance in the absence of a formal written constitution. A.V. Dicey saw the rule of law as a set of accepted guiding principles (*Introduction to the Study of the Law of the Constitution*, 10th edn, 1959, p.202). These were:

- the absolute supremacy or predominance of regular law as opposed to the influence of arbitrary power and exclusion of the existence of arbitrariness, of prerogative or even wide discretionary authority on the part of Government . . . a man may be punished for breach of the law but he cannot be punished for anything else;
- equality before the law, or the equal subjection of all classes to the ordinary law of the land and administered by the ordinary courts;
- the constitution as the result of the ordinary law of the land . . . the rights of the individual are secured by and enmeshed in the common law and not by a constitutional document which can be suspended by a stroke of the pen.

> **Key elements of the rule of law**
> - no-one should be able to justify their actions because of who they are but only with reference to their legal powers;
> - no-one is above the law;
> - laws should be transparent and certain, power should not be exercised in an arbitrary manner;
> - everyone is presumed innocent until proven guilty and has a right to a fair trial;
> - there is a strong and independent legal profession and judiciary.

To what extent are these principles reflected in English law?

Our courts have always accepted the need for officials to point to the source of their powers (*Entick v Carrington*, (KB, 1765)). Actions cannot be justified simply because they are acting in an official capacity. Lord Denning in *Gouriet v Union of Post Office Workers* (CA, 1977) famously said "Be you ever so high, the law is above you."

In many respects, however, the law does not match up to these strictures. A range of arbitrary powers is available to the Government under emergency powers and anti-terrorism legislation. Many government actions are still carried out by virtue of the royal prerogative, the limitations of which are difficult to define, although the courts are now prepared to control their exercise (*Council for Civil Service Unions v Minister for the Civil Service* (HL, 1984) see Ch.3. Governments exercise wide discretionary powers. Indeed it is difficult to see how any modern government could operate without its use. However, the rule of law does alert us to the need to ensure that discretionary power is properly controlled and our courts have recognised that discretionary power is never "unfettered" (e.g. *Padfield v Minister of Agriculture* (HL, 1968).

No one can be detained without proper legal authority.

Sometimes that authority is present in circumstances where no breach of the law has been established. An obvious example is the refusal of bail. Control orders under the Prevention of Terrorism Act 2005 and arbitrary powers of stop and search without the need for reasonable suspicion appear outside the spirit of the rule of law and must be closely monitored.

No one should be above the law and the law should apply to officials and citizens alike.

The privileges and immunities given to the Crown have tended to decrease over the years. The Crown Proceedings Act 1947 made it considerably easier to sue the Crown. Certain privileges and immunities remain: the personal immunity of the sovereign from being sued; the privilege of free speech granted to MPs; and diplomatic immunity. The trend in recent years has been for the development of a more coherent system of administrative law in England, a distinct procedure for raising public law issues by way of applications for judicial review and the establishment of the Administrative Court developing consistent principles of public law.

Commentators including Dicey clearly felt that stronger protection was given to constitutional rights by the ordinary law of the land than by a single constitutional document. Spreading the elements of the constitution limits the opportunity of a block repeal, for example. Many of an individual's constitutional rights now come from the ECHR by virtue of the **HRA**.

Limitations of the concept

The emphasis is on the regularity and certainty of the legal rules rather than on the content of the rules although Dicey does stress that decisions must be taken in accordance with procedural fairness. Nevertheless he is more concerned with regular enforcement and application rather than content. Other writers have attempted to expand the concept by including such matters as guarantees of economic prosperity and freedom from hunger (Delhi Declaration of the International Commission of Jurists 1959).

Conclusions on rule of law

The significance of the rule of law was emphasised by its inclusion in s.1 of the Constitutional Reform Act 2005 and by the many references to its importance by judges. Adherence to the rule of law may provide a check on abuse of power. It may provide a focus for critical evaluation of the way in which power is exercised. It is not itself a comprehensive code but must be supplemented by other principles which regulate the content of the legal rules themselves. The rule of law is not directly enforceable by the courts and there is no legal sanction for behaviour which contravenes it. It is best thought of as a guiding principle.

THE SUPREMACY OF PARLIAMENT

An important characteristic of the UK constitution has been that Parliament, not the constitution, was the supreme legal authority. While, in the majority of states, the legislature is limited by the constitution in what it can or cannot do, Westminster Parliament has been subject to no such legal limitation. Our courts have had no power to declare laws duly passed by Parliament invalid.

According to Blackstone "What Parliament doth, no power upon earth can undo." (*Commentaries on the Laws of England*, 1867 p.117). "In theory," said Dicey, "Parliament has total power. It is sovereign."

Dicey's view of Parliamentary supremacy
- Parliament was competent to pass laws on any subject.
- Its laws could regulate the activities of anyone, anywhere.
- Parliament could not bind its successors as to the content, manner and form of subsequent legislation.
- Laws passed by Parliament could not be challenged in the courts.

The legal limitations on the scope of Parliament's power

Dicey argued that there was no legal limitation on the scope of Parliament's power. Indeed Parliament has legislated on matters affecting every aspect of our lives. It has legislated to change fundamental constitutional principles. It has lengthened and shortened its own life. It has not even felt bound by territorial or jurisdictional limits. Parliament has legislated regarding aliens, even with regard to their activities outside British territory (The Hijacking Act 1967). Sir Ivor Jennings once said "If it [Parliament] enacts that smoking in the streets of Paris is an offence then, it is an offence." (*The Law and the Constitution*, 1963 p.170) There may be practical difficulties in enforcing such a law but that would not make it invalid.

Political considerations may make it unlikely that Parliament might legislate in a particular manner. Can one imagine a situation where Parliament passed legislation regulating the internal affairs of the United States? This led Professor H.W.R. Wade to argue that it was nonsensical to have a legal theory that Parliament could pass laws on any subject without restriction (Hamlyn lectures). Certainly there are many internal and external political limitations on Parliament's freedom of action.

It is now clear that British membership of the EU imposes a legal not simply a political limitation on Parliament. The **European Communities Act 1972** s.2(1) gives present and future community law legal force in the United Kingdom and s.2(2) provides for the implementation of community law by means of secondary legislation but the Act does not specifically prohibit Parliament from enacting conflicting legislation.

If, however, such conflicting legislation was ineffective in so far as it was inconsistent with community law, Parliament's power to legislate as it liked would be accordingly limited. Is it possible to argue that such a limitation has occurred as Parliament's authority to legislate has become integrated with EC legislative policy? Certainly, in practical terms, the increased co-operation required in the development of a common foreign and defence policy arising out of the Treaty on European Union and the emphasis on co-operation in home affairs is an ever increasing fetter on the Westminster Parliament's freedom of action.

The power of Parliament to bind its successors

The courts have long accepted Dicey's view that Parliament has no power to bind its successors either as to the manner or as to the form of subsequent legislation. As each successive Parliament is deemed to be all powerful, logically that Parliament must have the power to make or unmake any law. Accordingly it would seem to be impossible to entrench a provision in our constitution.

It was said in *Godden v Hales* (KB, 1686) that Parliament was entitled to ignore any provision in an earlier Act purporting to prevent the Act being repealed in the normal way, that is either expressly or by implication. This was followed in the case of *Ellen Street Estates Ltd v The Minister of Health* (CA, 1934) where the court found that it was impossible for Parliament to enact that in a subsequent statute dealing with the same subject matter, there should be no implied repeal. "The one thing Parliament cannot do is to bind its successor" (Maughan L.J.).

Various arguments have been put forward to suggest that specific statutory provisions have been entrenched.

The Statute of Westminster: Independence Acts

It has been argued that these have been entrenched as, in terms of the political realities of the situation, it is inconceivable that Parliament would repeal them (Lord Denning M.R. in *Blackburn v The Att-Gen* (CA, 1971)). That is not to say that if, in the future, Parliament did repeal an Independence Act and passed legislation purporting to regulate the internal affairs of the country, the British courts would reject such legislation. In *Madzimbamuto v Lardner Burke* (PC, 1969) Lord Reid said that even if Parliament acted improperly or unwisely, it was not open to the courts to say that it had acted illegally and that the resultant legislation was invalid. The court advised that a detention order made under the authority of an Emergency Powers Act passed by the illegal regime in Rhodesia was invalid as that regime's authority to legislate had been taken away. It did not allow the political reality of the situation to affect its conclusion knowing full well that the detention order would continue to be upheld within Rhodesia. In practical terms it was impossible to provide a remedy for the detained Madzimbamuto.

Where a sovereign state has been created by a grant of independence, the courts may be more reluctant to take back power in that they would have to recognise the political fact that the state in question was a foreign country and no longer part of the legal order of this country. Yet within our legal system, Parliament appears to have the legal power to repeal any law, even to act contrary to the principles of international law. The courts would simply uphold the latest intention of Parliament (see Lord Sankey in *British Coal Corp v The King* (HL, 1935) and Sir Robert Megarry in *Manuel v Att-Gen* (HC, 1983)).

The European Communities Act 1972

Several grounds have been suggested for holding that this Act cannot be repealed:

(a) That by joining the European Economic Community, a new order was created. Within that new order Parliament is no longer all powerful and cannot amend or repeal any statute by which that order was established. The **European Communities Act**, it is argued, is such a constituent statute, and is accordingly entrenched. A similar argument has been used with regard to the **Act of Union between Scotland and England in 1707.** (Note the EU Bill in 2010–11.)

(b) That by assigning rights and powers to the community in accordance with the Treaty provisions, Member States have limited their sovereign rights in such a way as to make it impossible to withdraw unilaterally (*Commission v Italy (Art Treasures)* Case (EC, 1972)).

   There is no evidence to suggest that the British courts would accept this view. Lord Denning in *Macarthy Ltd v Smith* (CA, 1979) clearly envisaged that Parliament could repeal the **1972 Act** although it would have to be done expressly and not by implication. The political view is clearly that a right to withdraw exists.

(c) That ultimately, the validity of legislation depends on the rules of recognition employed by our judges. The present norm of validity recognises the latest statutory intention of Parliament. It has been suggested that this norm has altered and that the courts will recognise as valid only legislation which has been passed by both houses and given the Royal Assent, has not been repealed expressly or by implication and which accords with our obligations under community law. Nevertheless, there remains a valid argument that the **European Communities Act** can be amended or repealed by Parliament, notwithstanding the obvious practical difficulties. The UK would not be able to remain a member of the European Union and careful consideration would have to be given to the plethora of primary and secondary legislation (e.g. on employment or agricultural matters) which are based on EU legislation.

KEY CASE

THOBURN V SUNDERLAND CITY COUNCIL (QB, 2001)
The applicants sold foodstuffs using imperial measures only. Legislation required metric measures to be used (albeit alongside imperial measures). The applicants were convicted under the **Weights and Measures Act 1985** (as amended by **Weights and Measures Act 1985 (Metrication) (Amendment) Order 1994**). Laws L.J. stated that the common law had come to recognise that there were certain fundamental constitutional rights and thus a hierarchy of Acts of Parliament, ordinary statutes and constitutional statutes. While ordinary statutes may be repealed by implication, the latter can only be repealed by express words on the face of the statute. The **European Communities Act** was such a statute.

Laws passed by Parliament cannot be challenged in the courts
Traditionally our courts have refused to consider the validity of an Act of Parliament either on the ground that Parliament had no power to pass it or on the ground that the statute had been improperly passed.

Substantive validity
Until the seventeenth century the courts would declare Acts of Parliament void if they considered them contrary to natural law, repugnant to the law or impossible to be performed. In modern times any such challenge has been totally unsuccessful.

In *R. v Jordan* (1967), Jordan, who had been sentenced for offences under the Race Relations Act 1965, applied for a writ of habeas corpus claiming that he had been convicted under an invalid law. He alleged that the statute in question was invalid in that it conflicted with a fundamental principle of natural law, the right of free speech. He claimed that no Act of Parliament could take away this right.

The argument was rejected by the court which simply stated that it had no power to consider the validity of an Act of Parliament. This view was endorsed by the House of Lords in *British Rail Board v Pickin* (HL, 1974) and followed in *Martin v O'Sullivan* (CA, 1982).

In order to maintain parliamentary supremacy the **HRA** does not give the courts any power to declare legislation invalid where it conflicts with the ECHR but simply allows the court to make a declaration of incompatibility (s.4). The onus is then on Parliament to change the law if it so wishes.

Procedural irregularity

Acts of Parliament have also been challenged on the ground that they have been improperly passed (see also Ch.7 judicial review). In 1842 a private Act of Parliament was challenged on this ground (*Edinburgh & Dalkeith Railway v Wauchope* (HL, 1842)). Lord Campbell, upholding the validity of the Act, refused to investigate the internal workings of Parliament saying that if the Act appeared valid on its face, then it must be accepted by the courts. If, from the Parliamentary Roll, it appeared that the Bill had passed through both Houses and received the Royal Assent, the courts could not inquire into what happened during its parliamentary stages. That is a question for Parliament.

A number of writers have sought to distinguish such a procedural challenge from the substantive challenge in cases such as *Jordan* arguing that it does not seek to limit Parliament's area of power. It can be argued that there is a clear difference between finding that Parliament has failed to follow its own procedural rules and from saying that Parliament does not have the power to legislate in a particular way. R.F.V. Heuston summarises this by saying that there is a distinction between the rules which govern on the one hand the composition and the procedure and on the other hand, the area of power of a sovereign legislature (R.F.V. Heuston, *Essays in Constitutional Law*, 1964, p.6).

The Judicial Committee of the Privy Council appeared to give some support to this distinction. In *Att-Gen for New South Wales v Trethowan* (PC, 1932) a decision of the Australian Supreme Court to grant a declaration that two Bills passed by the New South Wales State Legislature were invalid and grant an injunction restraining the Bills from being presented to the Governor for assent was upheld. The Privy Council found that the State Legislature was bound by s.5 of the Colonial Laws Validity Act 1865 which required any constitutional amendment to be in the manner and form required by the legislation in force at the time. The two Bills in question were not in the manner and form required as under earlier State legislation any constitutional change had to be approved by a referendum. But the House of Lords in *Pickin's* case (above) clearly rejected any sort of challenge to validity.

In *Jackson & Others v Her Majesty's Government* (HL, 2005), the court was prepared to consider the validity of the Hunting Act 2004 which had been forced through Parliament using the provisions of the **Parliament Act 1949**. It was argued that this Act was invalid having itself been passed using the earlier **Parliament Act 1911**. Although the court upheld the validity of these Acts, it was prepared to consider the question as it involved construction of the provisions of the Parliament Acts and not, as in *Pickin*, any investigation into the internal workings of Parliament.

00

0

0

MEMBERSHIP OF THE EU—ITS EFFECT ON PARLIAMENTARY SUPREMACY

In the view of the European Court, the courts of the Member States should give supremacy to Community law (*Costa v ENEL*, ECJ, 1964).

Section 2(4) European Communities Act

The 1967 White Paper on membership at para.23 states the Government's intention to be that "Community law takes precedence over the domestic law of the member states." Such an approach is essential to ensure the necessary harmonisation of the laws of the Member States.

Section 2(4) of the Act provides "... any enactment passed or to be passed, other than one contained in this Part of this Act, shall be construed and have effect subject to the foregoing provisions of this section ...". This refers back to s.2(1) which incorporates Community law into UK laws. Section 2(4) could therefore be said to give supremacy to Community law. But it can also be held to mean no more than it creates a presumption that, if there is a conflict between Community and domestic law, any ambiguity in that domestic law will be resolved to give effect to our Community obligations.

Initially the English courts took the view that English law and Community law were of equal status and that, by the doctrine of implied repeal, the courts should give effect to whatever represented the latest intention of Parliament e.g. *Bulmer (HP) Ltd v J Bollinger SA* (CA, 1974). Indeed on many occasions the approach was to avoid the problem altogether by treating s.2(4) simply as a principle of construction. So in *Garland v BR Engineering Co* (HL, 1983), an alleged conflict between s.6(4) of the **Sex Discrimination Act 1975** and the then Art.119 of the Treaty and subsequent directives was resolved by construing the Act widely (see also the approach in *Duke v GEC Reliance* (HL, 1988) and *Pickstone v Freemans Plc* (HL, 1989)).

Even where the courts indicated that priority should be given to Community law, they attempted to uphold the traditional view on sovereignty by arguing that Community law "is not supplanting English law. It is part of our law which overrides any other part which is inconsistent with it" (per Lord Denning M.R. in *Macarthys v Smith* (CA, 1981)). But where there is clear indication that Parliament did not intend to fulfil its obligations under the Treaty and intentionally and expressly acted inconsistently with it, Lord Denning felt it was the duty of the courts to follow the domestic statutes.

The courts seem finally to have accepted a modification of Dicey's approach in *R. v The Secretary of State for Transport, Ex p. Factortame Ltd* (HL, 1990).

The *Factortame* saga

Following the introduction of fishing quotas by the EC, Britain attempted to protect the interest of its fishermen by enacting the Merchant Shipping Act 1988. This prevented foreign nationals from securing part of the British quota by quota-hopping, for example by registering a company in this country. A number of Spanish fishermen who had been utilising part of the British quota by such methods challenged the validity of the **Merchant Shipping Act** on the grounds that it violated their rights under Community law. A preliminary ruling was requested under then Art.177 EC. In the meantime they applied for interim relief. The House of Lords in *Factortame 1* (1989) refused to grant interim relief (see Ch.8). It did, however, recognise that if the European Court ruled in favour of the applicants, the English courts would have to find a remedy and this might mean refusing to apply the provisions of the **Merchant Shipping Act**. On a further reference (*Factortame 2* (1991)), the Court of Justice reiterated the well established principle of Community law that a national court must set aside a domestic law which prevented Community law from having full effect. The matter then came back to the House of Lords in 1990. On this occasion their Lordships granted interim relief to prevent the Act being enforced on the basis that the applicants had shown a strong prima facie case and the other grounds for granting interim relief had been met.

Thus the House of Lords had effectively suspended the operation of the **Merchant Shipping Act** by accepting that, where there was a conflict, Community law must prevail. By granting interim relief against the Crown they had further ignored the **Crown Proceedings Act 1947** which preserved the common law rule which precluded the granting of such relief.

In the subsequent Scottish case of *Murray v Rogers* (1992) the Court of Session refused to challenge the validity of the Scottish community charge legislation, saying they had normally no power to consider whether an Act of Parliament was valid unless it was incompatible with Community law.

In *R. v Secretary of State for Employment Ex p. EOC* (HL, 1994), Lord Keith said that the effect of the *Factortame* decisions was that certain provisions of UK primary legislation could be held to be invalid in their purported application to nationals of Member States of the EU.

Factortame 1 did, however, leave open the question raised by Lord

Denning M.R. in *Macarthy* as to whether the British Parliament retained the power to legislate expressly in contravention of British treaty obligations. The effectiveness of any such legislation will, however, be limited. In *Jackson & Others v HMG* (HL, 2005), Lord Hope suggests that although Parliament has not specifically said that it would not pass legislation contrary to Community law, that is, in practice, the effect of s.2(1) when read with s.2(4) of the Act.

THE HUMAN RIGHTS ACT AND SUPREMACY

Lord Steyn in *R. v DPP Ex p. Kebilene* (HL, 2000) said that this carefully and subtly drafted Act preserves the principles of parliamentary sovereignty. That clearly was the intention of Parliament. There is no equivalent power to that of s.2(4) of the **European Communities Act 1972**. The courts cannot declare any law invalid for being in conflict with the convention. Rather, under s.4 the superior courts can make a declaration of incompatibility where a provision of primary or subordinate legislation is not convention compliant. This does not, of itself, affect the validity of the legislation nor is it binding on the parties to the instant case. A number of such declarations have now been made, for example in *A(FC) & Others v Secretary of State for the Home Department* (HL, 2004) where the Anti-terrorism, Crime and Security Act 2001 s.23 was incompatible with arts 5 and 14. This led to the introduction and modification of control orders for terrorist suspects who have not been charged with offences yet whom are deemed a danger to the public.

Following a finding of incompatibility government ministers can use a fast track procedure in s.10 to amend the law by using subordinate legisla-tion. While not without precedent, the power to amend primary legislation by ministerial order is highly unusual and some critics have said that it sets a dangerous precedent which could lead to a considerable increase in executive power.

Section 19 shows that Parliament can legislate contrary to the con-vention. But it has been argued that the rule of interpretation laid down in s.3(1) which requires the court, so far as it is possible to do so, to read and give effect to legislation in a way which is compatible with convention rights, goes much further than existing rules of statutory interpretation and repre-sents a challenge to parliamentary supremacy. In *R. v A* (HL, 2002) the court "read down" (arguably distorting the meaning of) the provision to ensure the accused received a fair trial. In *Antonio Mendoza v Ahmad Raja Ghaidan* (HL, 2004) the court departed from an earlier interpretation of a statutory provi-sion relating to the tenancy rights of spouses. As they now had to take into account Convention rights they re-interpreted the section to give the same sex partner of a deceased tenant the right to remain in the property.

The extent to which the courts have been prepared to use their power under s.3(1) has appeared to vary. In *Ghaidan* the court warned that it should not go against the grain of the legislation by contradicting its essential purpose, nor take decisions of wide social or economic importance that should be left to Parliament. But Lord Steyn cautioned against overuse of s.4 powers and felt they should be more willing to use s.3. Has the correct balance been struck to maintain the supremacy of Parliament?

Revision checklist

You should now know and understand:

- **the nature of the British constitution;**
- **the sources of the British Constitution;**
- **the rule of law;**
- **the concept of parliamentary supremacy.**

QUESTION AND ANSWER

The Question

"Parliament has under the English constitution, the right to make or unmake any law whatever; and no person or body is recognised by the law of England as having a right to override or set aside the legislation of Parliament."

To what extent does this traditional (Diceyean) view retain relevance in light of the UK's membership of the European Union and Council of Europe?

Advice and the Answer

Essay questions must be read carefully and the answer structured so as to directly answer the question set. Lecturers cannot usually give marks for material which although accurate is not relevant to the question.

In this instance, there are three main elements which must be addressed: the Diceyean view, as illustrated by the quote, the impact of EU law and the impact of the Council of Europe membership (and thus the **European Convention on Human Rights**). Given the quote, the focus must be on whether Parliament can "make or unmake any law" and whether any other body can "override or set aside" parliamentary legislation. The powers of national courts, the European Court of Justice (and other organs) and the European Court of Human Rights may thus be considered.

This is essentially a rather broad (and common) question on parliamentary supremacy.

1. Explanation of Dicey's traditional view
Parliament can make laws on any subject affecting anyone, anywhere.

The courts must give effect to the latest intention of Parliament—there is no hierarchy of laws.

The courts have no power to challenge the validity of an Act of Parliament (*British Rail Board v Pickin* (HL, 1974)).

2. Consideration of whether Parliament still has freedom of action to make or unmake any law

(i) Note the effect of membership of the EU.
The view of the ECJ is that, by joining the EU, Member States have limited their sovereign rights (*Costa v ENEL* (1964)). Under the treaty obligations, within those areas regulated by Community law Member States have obligations to reconcile domestic law with Community law and their courts must give effect to Community law.

If Parliament makes laws which are contrary to Community law, even if they represent the latest intention of Parliament, on the authority of *Factortame*, UK courts will now give effect to Community law. They have accepted that s.2(4) has created a hierarchy of laws in the sense that it clearly prevents Parliament repealing Community law by implication and that they have the power to disapply an Act of Parliament (The **Crown Proceedings Act**) to ensure the claimant can exercise his rights under Community law. On whether Parliament has the power to repeal Community law expressly, or indeed the **1972 Act** itself-no clear authority. Discuss the argument that Parliament has redefined itself into a less than sovereign body, of relevance is Lord Denning's dicta in *Macarthys v Smith* and Laws L.J. in *Thoburn*.

(ii) Consideration of the Human Rights Act
The ECHR has not been fully incorporated into UK law in the same way as Community law. It should be noted that Parliament still retains the right to legislate contrary to the Convention. The **HRA** simply imposes an obligation to declare whether the legislation is compliant or not.

Nevertheless it imposes a significant moral and political pressure on governments to comply. In addition s.3(1) of the **HRA** requires the court to adopt an approach to interpretation which might require the judge to ignore the intention of Parliament in order to construe the provision in a way which accords with the Convention. Discuss the extent to which the courts have been prepared to read down legislation with reference to cases such as *R. v A*, *Bellinger v Bellinger* and *Ghaidan*.

3. Conclusion

Dicey's concept of supremacy must clearly be modified in the light of the above. *Factortame* has shown the extent the courts are prepared to go in ensuring the supremacy of Community law. However it must be noted that as yet the courts have not been required to declare an Act invalid for being contrary to Community law. They have no power to declare legislation invalid in contexts other than Community law. Under the **HRA** the courts have no power to declare legislation invalid but can only issue a declaration of incompatibility. It is then up to the Government to act if they so wish.

The Executive

3

INTRODUCTION

The executive is responsible for the initiation, formulation, direction and implementation of general government policy. As will be described below, decisions are taken by the Cabinet and implemented by the various government departments, each headed by a government minister. Historically these powers derived from the Crown but today the monarch plays no real part in the process of government.

This chapter will consider the following:

- the role of the monarch under the constitution and the powers exercised by, or in the name of, the monarch;
- the doctrine of separation of powers, which refers to the relationship between the organs of State (executive, legislature and judiciary);
- the constitutional role of the cabinet and the doctrine of ministerial responsibility for decisions taken by the executive;
- mechanisms for accessing official information and the circumstances in which such information can be withheld.

Nowadays the source of much power is the legislative authority of Parliament expressed through acts of Parliament. Ministers are constitutionally answerable to Parliament for the conduct of their departments.

THE MONARCH

The monarch is described as a constitutional monarch. She is Head of State, Head of the Commonwealth, Head of the Armed Forces and provides a focus for national unity. She performs a number of formal constitutional functions, giving the Royal Assent to legislation, opening the new Parliament, appointing the Prime Minister and a host of senior government and other public appointments. In practice however, she has no real power as she is required to act on the advice of her Prime Minister. The last monarch to refuse to grant the Royal Assent to legislation was Queen Anne. Only a few honours remain in the personal grant of the sovereign.

Those areas where she appears to have some residual power, such as the appointment of the Prime Minister, are illusory as she is entirely restricted by the convention that she approaches the leader of the party with the largest number of seats in Parliament and the parties themselves have now clearly defined methods of selecting their leader. Some political influence may remain in the power to grant or refuse a dissolution of Parliament. It is argued that in the most exceptional circumstances the monarch could thereby influence events. The 2007 White Paper, The Governance of Britain, proposes certain changes in the convention relating to dissolution of Parliament. It recommended that the Prime Minister should be obliged to seek the approval of the House of Commons before approaching the monarch to request a dissolution, but this was not enacted in the resulting Constitutional Reform and Governance Act 2010. However, the coalition Government has announced its intention to impose fixed five-year terms on Parliament (the Fixed-Term Parliaments Bill).

Walter Bagehot writing in the nineteenth century said that the monarch had the right to be consulted, the right to encourage and the right to warn. Prime Ministers have a weekly audience with the Queen. She receives foreign heads of state and ambassadors. She is supplied with copies of all cabinet papers and minutes, important Foreign Office telegrams and a summary of daily events in Parliament. Many Prime Ministers have indicated that they value the Queen's vast experience although the extent to which there is influence must remain a matter for future historians.

THE POWERS AND FUNCTIONS OF THE STATE

The state has three types of function: legislative, judicial and executive. The legislative function is exercised mainly through Parliament which has the power to make laws of general applicability and to grant other bodies the power to make delegated legislation under authority of an Act of Parliament. Originally the monarch had the power to make laws by means of royal proclamation. A residue of this is the power to make orders in council.

The state also has the authority to determine disputes which arise out of the operation of its laws. Such disputes are allocated to courts, tribunals or even to government ministers, who increasingly exercise functions of a judicial nature. No clear principles determine the allocation of disputes to these bodies although the greater the element of discretion and the more important the policy considerations, the less likely it is for the courts to take on the new area of responsibility.

The state has various executive functions. It must initiate, formulate and direct general policy. That policy must then be put into operation, monitored and regulated. Responsibility for this is with the government of the country, the main decisions being taken by the Cabinet and put into effect by the various government departments and a range of quasi-autonomous bodies.

Figure 3.1: Powers and functions of the State

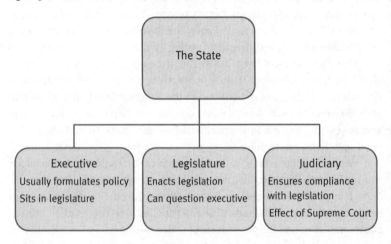

The doctrine of separation of powers

Writers, as long ago as Aristotle, have been concerned that if legislative, executive and judicial functions were concentrated in the same person or body, that body would become too powerful and would abuse its power. To avoid this they have argued that power should be distributed. One way of achieving this is by the doctrine of separation of powers where, for example, all legislative powers are concentrated in one body, all judicial powers in another and so on. Each body would then be strong enough to check and balance the power of the others. The most famous exponent of this doctrine was the eighteenth-century French writer, Montesquieu. In fact his observations on the then British system of government over-emphasised the degree of separation.

There has never been a strict separation of powers in the UK. Unlike the United States, the Prime Minister and the Cabinet are drawn from Parliament. Although Parliament is the main legislative organ, the courts and the

Figure 3.2: Separation of powers: each organ can act as a check on the other organs

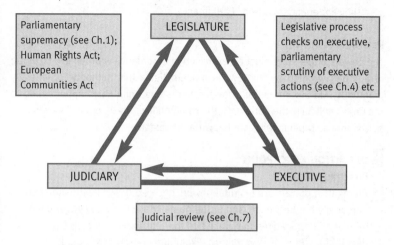

Parliamentary supremacy (see Ch.1); Human Rights Act; European Communities Act

LEGISLATURE

Legislative process checks on executive, parliamentary scrutiny of executive actions (see Ch.4) etc

JUDICIARY

EXECUTIVE

Judicial review (see Ch.7)

executive both have legislative responsibilities (interpretation, initiation). Government ministers have legislative, executive and judicial functions.

Indeed it is extremely difficult to establish any truly satisfactory system of defining the limits of these functions. Rather they seem to merge. Yet it has proved necessary to attempt this task to determine the appropriate checks and balances in the system. The courts' attitude to intervention to control any abuse of power is affected by the nature of the power being exercised (see *Re Racal Communications Ltd* (HL, 1981) and *Vine v National Dock Labour Board* (HL, 1957).

The doctrine is, however, of particular value in that it helps to maintain the independence of the judiciary. The effect of the **Human Rights Act 1998** has also been to point to the need for an independent judiciary (*Findlay v UK* (ECHR, 1997) and see also Ch.7) and there have been a series of cases challenging the independence of those exercising judicial functions. In *McGonnell v UK* (ECHR, 2000) it was found that the dual role of the Bailiff of Guernsey in approving the development plan for the area and hearing an appeal in relation to the planning process, cast doubt on his impartiality as a judge. This focused concern on the role of the then Lord Chancellor as presiding officer in the House of Lords, a government minister and member of the Cabinet and a judge, and has led to significant constitutional changes:

- the Lord Chancellor has ceased to be head of the judiciary and presiding officer in the House of Lords;
- an independent judicial appointments system, set up under the Constitutional Reform Act 2003;
- the establishment of a Supreme Court with the Law Lords moving out of

the House of Lords in 2009 to separate premises thereby emphasising their independence from Parliament.

Prerogative power

The powers of the state must be exercised in accordance with the law by virtue of authority granted by the law. In modern times this authority is generally granted by statute but certain powers, rights and immunities appertaining to the Crown still have their origins in the common law. These, originally exercised by the monarch personally, are known as prerogative powers.

▌ DEFINITION CHECKPOINT

Prerogative powers

Prerogative powers are residual powers once exercised by the monarch personally but now exercised in the name of the Crown by government ministers. Prerogatives may relate to the legislative, executive or judicial functions of government. Examples of prerogatives still in existence include: the administration of overseas territories by means of orders in council; authority to make treaties; the recognition of foreign states; declarations of war; the disposition and control of the armed forces; the organisation of the civil service; power to take action in an emergency; the prerogative of mercy; the power to stop criminal prosecutions; the granting of the Royal Assent to legislation; the summoning and dissolution of Parliament and the grant of Honours.

The prerogative is a residual power and will be superseded by statute (See *R. v Home Secretary, Ex p. Fire Brigades Union* (HL, 1995).) Where the statutory provision deals with the same area, the prerogative may be extinguished either expressly or by implication (see *Att-Gen v De Keyser's Royal Hotel* (HL, 1920) but cf. *R. v Home Secretary, Ex p. Northumbria Police Authority* (CA, 1988)).

Following the decision of then Prime Minister Tony Blair to commit troops to Iraq in 2003, there have been a number of legal challenges to the prerogative of war. In addition, the Chilcot enquiry is reviewing the evidentiary base for that particular use of prerogative powers.

▌ KEY CASE

R (GENTLE) V PRIME MINISTER (HL, 2008)

The claimants were the mothers of two 19-year-old soldiers who had died in Iraq during the UK military action instigated in 2003.

"Article 2 of the [European] Convention imposes a duty on member states to protect life. This duty extends to the lives of

soldiers. Armed conflict exposes soldiers to the risk of death. Therefore a state should take timely steps to obtain reliable legal advice before committing its troops to armed conflict. Had the UK done this before invading Iraq in March 2003, it would arguably not have invaded. Had it not invaded, [the soldiers] would not have been killed."
(Lord Bingham at para.3 summarising the arguments).

The House of Lords unanimously dismissed the appeal, considering such a wide-ranging review of the decision to deploy military (the prerogative power) non-justiciable not least because the arguments submitted were based on the **Human Rights Act** (and the duty to investigate under Art.2 European Convention). Inquiries had already been held into the deaths of the soldiers. The claimants really wanted a full inquiry into the advice of the Attorney-General, something deemed legally unarguable.

The Chilcot (Iraq) enquiry subsequently was established in 2009 to consider "the UK's involvement in Iraq, including the way decisions were made and actions taken, to establish, as accurately as possible, what happened and to identify the lessons that can be learned." At the time of writing, it is still sitting (see *http://www.iraqinquiry.org.uk*).

In the past the courts were reluctant to interfere with prerogative powers. In *Laker Airways v Department of Trade* (HC, 1976) the court indicated that while it would determine the existence and the scope of the prerogative power, it would not review the propriety or adequacy of the grounds on which it had been exercised. However in *Council for Civil Service Unions v Minister for the Civil Service* (HL, 1984)(see Ch.7), the House of Lords recognised the possibility of reviewing the exercise of prerogative power on the same grounds as power granted under statutory provisions. It rationalised this by saying that nowadays the question of whether a power was authorised by statute or prerogative was largely a matter of historical accident. This was further recognised in cases such as *R. v Secretary of State for the Home Department Ex p. Fire Brigades Union* (HL, 1995) and *R. v Home Secretary Ex p. Bentley* (HC, 1994) where the court was willing to review the Home Secretary's exercise of the prerogative of mercy. However, as can be seen in Ch.7, the courts will often consider the subject matter of the decision they are asked to review inappropriate for judicial intervention and therefore non justiciable. In *Abbasi v Foreign Secretary* (CA, 2002) the Court of Appeal refused to query prerogative powers for dealing with foreign states (in this case making representations to the USA on detention of Abassi's son at Guantanamo Bay).

THE CABINET AND THE PRIME MINISTER

All major government decisions are taken by the Cabinet.

DEFINITION CHECKPOINT
The cabinet
The cabinet is a committee of senior government ministers. In the UK, it is for the Cabinet to determine the policies to be submitted to Parliament, to determine the content and priorities of legislative proposals, and to ensure that the relevant policies are carried out.

By convention all members of the Cabinet are collectively responsible for decisions taken. While the matter is under discussion ministers can air their views but once the matter is decided all members of the Government, whether within the Cabinet or not, must support it. If they are unable to do this then they should resign as Michael Heseltine did during the Westland affair and Robin Cook over the invasion of Iraq. The force with which this convention is observed has varied with the political climate. Indeed it was formally suspended during the campaign prior to the referendum on continuing membership of the EU.

There are no rules prescribing the size of the Cabinet and increasingly the Cabinet operates through a network of committees, the result being that ministers may be bound by decisions in which they have had little more than nominal participation.

As with the Cabinet itself, the office of Prime Minister is one which is barely recognised in law. The twentieth century saw a steady increase in the powers of the Prime Minister who is now in a very strong position.

- As leader of the party in power, he has been chosen by the electorate, has control over the party machinery and can normally rely on the strength of party loyalty to maintain his position. His public profile is higher than that of any other minister.
- As chairman of the Cabinet, he can to a large extent determine the nature of discussions within the Cabinet. Matters can be referred to sub-committees and the agenda manipulated to ensure the desired result.
- As ultimate head of the civil service, the Prime Minister has powers over senior appointments and access to all information.
- The Cabinet Office, although technically providing a service for all members of the Cabinet, has grown into the Prime Minister's special source of assistance and information.
- The Prime Minister is the source of much patronage. He appoints and dismisses government ministers and has at his disposal a wide selection of public appointments, honours, etc.

It is, however, wrong to think of the Prime Minister as having absolute power. However dominant, s/he must keep the support of his/her party both inside and outside Parliament. Ultimately the Prime Minister is dependent on continued party support, as well as the support of the electorate—this is something carefully negotiated for the 2010 onwards Conservative and Liberal Democrat coalition. It is already proving problematic in respect of welfare reform and, in England, raising university tuition fees (the latter explicitly contrary to Liberal Democrat pre-election policy).

Government ministers and departments

Functioning of the coalition

"Close consultation between the Prime Minister and Deputy Prime Minister, other Ministers and members of the Conservative and Liberal Democrat Parties in both Houses will be the foundation of the Coalition's success. In the working of the coalition, the principle of balance will underpin both the coalition parties' approaches to all aspects of the conduct of the Government's business, including the allocation of responsibilities, the Government's policy and legislative programme, the conduct of its business and the resolution of disputes.

1. Composition of the Government

1.1 The initial allocation of Cabinet, Ministerial, Whip and Special Adviser appointments between the two Parties was agreed between the Prime Minister and the Deputy Prime Minister.

1.2 Future allocation will continue to be based on the principle that the Parliamentary Party with fewer MPs will have a share of Cabinet, Ministerial and Whip appointments agreed between the Prime Minister and the Deputy Prime Minister, approximately in proportion to the size of the two Parliamentary parties. The Prime Minister, following consultation with the Deputy Prime Minister, will make nominations for the appointment of Ministers. The Prime Minister will nominate Conservative Party Ministers and the Deputy Prime Minister will nominate Liberal Democrat Ministers. The Prime Minister and the Deputy Prime Minister will agree the nomination of the Law Officers."

(*Coalition Agreement for Stability and Reform*, May 2010)

The various tasks undertaken by central government are executed by government departments such as the Treasury, the Home Office and the Foreign Office. The organisation and responsibilities of these vary from time to time. At the head of each is a government minister, normally assisted by several junior ministers. Each minister will have a Parliamentary Private Secretary. By convention these will all be members of Parliament although not necessarily from the House of Commons. There is no legal limit on the number of ministers but there is a limit on the number who can sit and vote in the Commons (House of Commons Disqualification Act 1975, s.2(1)), presently 95, and a limit to the number of ministerial salaries which can be paid (Ministerial and other Salaries Act 1975). Under the Ministerial and other Salaries Act 1997, ministerial salaries are linked to those of civil servants. (Note the Conservative–Liberal Democrat coalition announced in May 2010 that all ministers were accepting a five per cent pay cut and a five-year pay freeze.)

The departments are staffed by professional civil servants, each one headed by a Permanent Secretary. Civil servants must serve whatever government is in power even if they are not in sympathy with that government's views. To ensure this impartiality there are stringent restrictions on the degree of political involvement permitted to civil servants.

Ministerial responsibility

By convention, ministers are responsible to Parliament for the conduct of their departments (*Carltona v Commissioner of Works* (CA, 1943)).

DEFINITION CHECKPOINT

Ministerial responsibility

Ministers may be legally responsible for the acts and omissions of their department and government agencies. They are accountable to Parliament which has the right to question the minister on any aspect of the work of the department, even regarding events prior to his taking office. The Ministerial Code (2005) reminds ministers of their duty to give accurate and truthful information to Parliament and to be as open as possible in accordance with the Code of Practice on Access to Government Information (1997) and with the **Freedom of Information Act 2000**. The degree of personal responsibility depends on the circumstances. The modern tendency is that the minister is not required to shelter a civil servant who has acted improperly, particularly if he has disobeyed instructions or failed to follow established procedures. Ministers can be held responsible in law (*M v Home Office* (HL, 1991)).

Ministers who feel personally to blame for an event will normally tender their resignation (e.g. David Laws in May 2010) but if a minister is merely criticised, no clear pattern emerges as to whether he will resign. Largely this is a political question depending on a number of factors such as the government's strength and the need to relieve pressure on it (see the work of Professor Dowding et al at the London School of Economics on ministerial resignations over the last century). Some would argue that the establishment of government agencies has made it easier for ministers to avoid taking responsibility for mistakes by seeking to blame the chief executive of an agency but it is sometimes difficult in practice to separate broad policy from day-to-day activities.

THE AVAILABILITY OF OFFICIAL INFORMATION

The traditional attitude of government was that official information should remain secret unless the government chooses to make it available. This was justified on security grounds but often the argument was that disclosure was not in the public interest. This position has altered significantly with the emphasis now on greater openness of government with transparency of process and freedom of information. Nevertheless, national security remains the most common ground for blocking information. The series of legal actions initiated by the Government to suppress publication of the memoirs of a former intelligence agent, Peter Wright, indicates the lengths to which the Government will go to ensure confidentiality. In *AG v Guardian Newspapers* (No. 2) (HL, 1988) it was accepted that the Crown had a right to attempt to restrain disclosure of confidential information relating to the operation of the security services but that they must establish that the disclosure was in some way damaging to the public interest. In view of the widespread publicity given to Peter Wright's book *Spycatcher* (including the legal publication of extracts in Scotland) it was felt that such damage could not now be established and the injunction against publication was discharged.

Cabinet discussions
The courts have protected the secrecy of cabinet discussions by granting injunctions and by refusing applications for discovery of documents. In *Att-Gen v Jonathan Cape Ltd* (HC, 1976) the court held that it had the power to restrain publication of material relating to such discussions although the power was not then exercised.

In *Conway v Rimmer* (HL, 1968) the need for secrecy was justified because:
- it ensured full and frank discussion within the Cabinet;
- it helped to preserve the convention of collective responsibility;
- it protected governments from ill-formed or captious criticism.

This is less than convincing and the suspicion exists that the true reason for secrecy is to protect governments against criticism. However, many former government ministers now publish "memoirs", often in the form of diaries which detail aspects of cabinet discussions (e.g. the range of memoirs published and about to be published on the "New Labour era" of government).

The Public Records Acts

The Public Records Acts 1958–75 protected cabinet documents and other government papers for 30 years, unless the Government chose to make them available. The period could be extended if continued secrecy was deemed to be in the public interest. Note the controversy over the evidence of the Hutton inquiry into the death of Dr David Kelly with non-evidentiary records submitted to the inquiry classified for 30 years and medical details including the post-mortem for 70 years. The Freedom of Information Act 2000 replaces the largely discretionary regime for access to public records with a new statutory regime and provides enhanced access to records more than 30 years old.

The Official Secrets Acts 1911–89

The overwhelming climate of secrecy was encouraged and supported by the Official Secrets Acts 1911–20 which were used not simply to prevent disclosure of security information but to prevent the disclosure of all information which governments chose not to disclose whether or not there were any national security implications.

The whole emphasis of the first **Act** in 1889 was on espionage and treason. The aim of the **1911 Act** was to strengthen the law against spying. In *Chandler v DPP* (HL, 1964), members of a group supporting nuclear disarmament were convicted under s.1 following an incident where they entered an RAF base and attempted to obstruct its use. This sabotage was held to fall within the conduct prohibited by s.1. The House of Lords held that the question whether the conduct was prejudicial to the interests of the state was for the court and not for the jury.

The Official Secrets Act 1989, is designed to protect more limited classes of official information. Section 1(1) thereof makes it an offence for any member or former member of the security and intelligence services to disclose information relating to, or in support of, these services. Where the disclosure is by a Crown servant or contractor, only those disclosures which are damaging to the public interest are criminalised. No such public interest defence is available to members of the security services charged under s.1(1) (see *R. v Shayler* (HL, 2001)).

In the case of disclosure of information on defence, international relations, crime, information resulting from unauthorised disclosures or entrusted in confidence by a crown servant, ss.2–5 make disclosure an offence if made without lawful authority and causing damage to the public interest. This is subject to the defence that the accused did not know the nature of the information or realise that its disclosure would be damaging.

The **1989 Act** did not include a "public interest" defence for "whistleblowers" who felt that the public should be told certain information. The Public Interest Disclosure Act 1998, which provides employees who make disclosures about wrong-doings in the workplace with some protection against victimisation by employers, does not apply to the armed forces or members of the security services.

Figure 3.3: Accessing official information

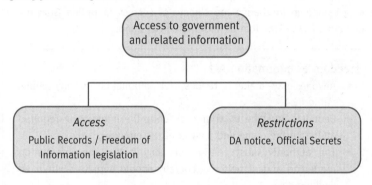

The "DA" notice system

In addition to the restrictions arising out of the **Official Secrets Acts**, the media is further restricted in what it can publish by a system of self-censorship known as the Defence Advisory ("DA") Notice System (see *http://www.dnotice.org.uk*). Much journalistic material is obtained from official sources "off the record". Because of the width of our official secrets legislation and the effect of laws on breach of confidence and contempt, the use of such information may constitute a breach of the law. Editors require some guidance as to whether action is likely to follow a particular disclosure. Prince Harry's 2007–8 deployment to Afghanistan was subject to a "DA" notice to protect him and the soldiers serving with him. This was broken by an Australian magazine in February 2008; the media "blackout" was adhered to by all UK media.

This informal guidance is given by the Defence, Press and Broadcasting Advisory Committee which is composed of civil servants and representatives of the media. It issues "DA" notices advising that those matters listed should not be published as they are required to remain secret for security reasons.

Categories of information presently covered include information about nuclear weapons installations, the British Intelligence Services and highly classified military information. Editors can submit individual stories to the Committee for guidance. It should be noted that any clearance is purely informal and does not give any immunity from prosecution. There have been occasions where, despite clearance being given by the Committee, the Government has sought an injunction restraining publication. Conversely, publication in breach of a "DA" notice is not, of itself, a criminal offence although the likelihood is that it will fall within the ambit of the legislation.

Freedom of information

Unless information about the workings of government is freely available, it is extremely difficult to call the government to account for its actions. There was a long campaign to change the climate of secrecy in British Government culminating in the **Freedom of Information Act 2000**.

Freedom of Information Act

- Anyone may make a request for information to any public authority.
- Requests must be in writing, describe the information required and state the name and answer of the enquirer.
- The authority must confirm or deny it has the information requested and, if held, it generally should supply it within 20 working days.
- There are absolute and qualified exemptions:
  - absolute exemptions include information already available through other means, security matters, confidential and personal information and parliamentary privilege matters;
  - qualified exemptions impose a duty on the authority to consider whether disclosure would be in the public interest and thus outweighs the exemption. Reasons for withholding the information must be given. This category includes international relations and foreign affairs, defence and communications with Her Majesty.
- A fee may be charged for the information.
- Publication schemes are now maintained (e.g. *http://www.nationalarchives.gov.uk/news/releases-archive.htm*).
- The Information Commissioner monitors and enforces the system.

The **Freedom of Information Act**, passed in 2000 introduced a general right of access to information held by a wide range of public authorities listed in

Sch.1 of the Act such as local and national government departments, the police, schools, universities and hospitals.

The Act is supplemented by Codes of Practice, which provide guidance on specific issues. Any request for information must be made in writing and the authority in question is entitled to charge a fee for providing the information. The information must be supplied within 20 working days unless there is a possible exemption and the public interest test is being applied. In such cases an estimate as to when a reply will be forthcoming must be given within the 20-day period.

Critics have argued that the legislation is defective in a number of ways. The list of exemptions is extremely wide. It is not always easy to see how these can be justified in the public interest. The Act does not create a right to obtain the documents themselves, only the information contained within them.

Revision Checklist

You should now know and understand:

- the role of the monarch;

- the doctrine of separation of powers;

- the role of the cabinet and Ministerial responsibility;

- the mechanisms for accessing official information.

QUESTION AND ANSWER

The Question

"The separation of powers is more a myth than reality in the United Kingdom". Assess the extent to which there is an appropriate separation of powers in the UK.

Advice and the Answer

This question clearly specifies the expectations for the answer: the answer must consider separation of powers, to what extent there is separation of powers in the UK and whether the British system is appropriate or not. A personal value judgement is thus required although, obviously, your viewpoint must be substantiated by supporting authority.

1. Separation of powers

It is necessary to demonstrate a basic understanding of the doctrine of separation of powers—what it is; the reasoning behind it; and possibly some history and background information. Note that a detailed historical description would not be expected and would not attract marks.

2. UK reality

The UK does not operate a strict separation of powers. The reality in the UK requires an explanation, describing the overlap in powers which exists in the UK. It would also be necessary to point out the mechanisms in the UK for ensuring there are sufficient checks and balances in place within the UK's constitutional framework. The Supreme Court and judicial appointment systems should be considered with respect to the independence of the judiciary. The role of the cabinet and overlap between executive and legislative functions may also be considered.

3. Evaluation

Given the question asks you to consider the "extent to which there is an appropriate separation of powers in the UK", you are expected to present your opinion and substantiate it with relevant authorities. It does not matter what your opinion is, as long as you can cite examples and authority thereon. It would be acceptable to use some examples from current affairs, if relevant, as well as examples studied in class. Perhaps you are familiar with other constitutional frameworks—if so, this could provide an interesting viewpoint for discussing the UK position (e.g. United States of America; Australia, China). Note also that this question lends itself to a detailed evaluation of several topics including parliamentary scrutiny of the executive (see Ch.4) and parliamentary supremacy (Ch.2). Scrutiny obviously relates to the checks and balance the legislature can exercise over the executive; parliamentary supremacy relates to the checks the judiciary can impose on the legislature. Judicial review (Ch.7) is also relevant insofar as it relates to the judiciary exercising a check on the powers of the executive. Therefore, this question has a broad range of topics from which you can draw your answer.

4. Conclusions

Your answer should conclude with a clear exposition of your view. In other words, a clear answer to the question posed. This should follow naturally from the discussion in your answer and thus, essentially, be a summary and final recapitulation of the key points.

Parliament

4

INTRODUCTION

Parliament is the principal legislature in the UK. It consists of three elements; the Monarch; the House of Commons; and the House of Lords. Although it can voluntarily relinquish power (e.g. through the **European Communities Act** to the EU, or through the devolution acts to the regional bodies), it retains supremacy, as discussed in Ch.2. Parliament also, in terms of separation of powers, exercises a check on the power of the executive through scrutiny of legislation and policies. An understanding of the constitutional role of parliament and its current powers and responsibilities includes consideration of:

- the composition of Parliament, its roles and its legal privileges;
- the legislative process and the various checks and balances on executive power therein;
- the implications of devolution on the power of Parliament;
- the mechanisms by which Parliament can question Executive policies and decision, holding the executive to account in terms of separation of powers.

THE COMPOSITION OF PARLIAMENT

Parliament consists of three elements (see *http://www.parliament.uk*):

- the Monarch;
- the House of Lords;
- the House of Commons.

The Monarch is self-explanatory, the others require further elaboration.

The House of Lords

This is currently a non-elected chamber. The **House of Lords Act 1999** instituted a process of reform of the upper chamber (still ongoing) and in 2000, the House of Lords Appointments Commission began work. This Commission verifies the suitability of all nominees and recommends non-political appointments to the Queen.

Figure 4.1

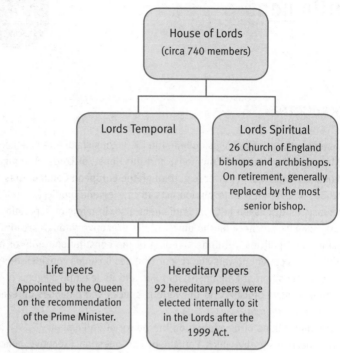

The role and composition of the House of Lords has been subject to considerable criticism, most commonly the fact that there are still some hereditary peers, and life peers are all too often political appointments. Moreover, there are arguments that it is wrong for an unelected body to impose even a limited check on the activities of an elected Government. Previous allegations of a conservative (political) bias have been ameliorated by a number of the reform innovations.

The work of the House of Lords

Nevertheless, the House of Lords does perform a number of useful functions:

1. *Legislative functions.*
   (a) A number of Bills, mainly non-controversial, start life in the Lords.
   (b) The House does a considerable amount of scrutiny of complex and technical legislation. Many Government amendments are brought in the Lords to save time in the Commons.
   (c) It bears the brunt of the examination of private Bills.
   (d) It does valuable work in the scrutiny of delegated legislation including European secondary legislation. Not only does this

save time in the Commons, it provides another type of less politically charged scrutiny by those who may have a wide range of expertise and experience.

2. *Debating function.* The House of Lords provides a useful forum for debating the great issues of the day.

3. *Check on government.* It is argued that in view of the impotence of the House of Commons and the flexibility of the British Constitution, it is necessary for there to be some check on the activities of Government. Although limited by the Parliament Acts and the convention of non-involvement in financial matters, the House of Lords is an important check. The Lords can publicise matters and delay action for long enough to allow public opinion to be developed and expressed.

Reform of the House of Lords

Completing the reforms initiated in 1999 has proved to be extremely difficult. Debate over the future of the House of Lords has centered on the need for a bicameral legislature and the composition of the House.

The need for a bicameral legislature: Given the substantial workload of the Commons, the legislative function of the House of Lords remains important. There are many examples of Bills proceeding to the Lords following limited scrutiny with considerable numbers of government amendments being brought in the Lords. It could be argued that what is needed is reform of the Commons to enable it to cope with the volume of work. There is, however, an argument that scrutiny and revision by a different chamber has value in bringing a different, less party political perspective.

A further justification for a second chamber is that it imposes a check on the House of Commons. We do not have a written constitution or a constitutional court to test the legitimacy of government action. In view of the Government's usual tight control of the Commons, a second chamber may have value.

The composition of the second chamber: There are clear concerns about an Upper House consisting largely of Government nominees. It would of course be possible to take the selection of life peers out of the hands of government and establish an independent commission, or indeed to have an elected chamber. An obvious difficulty of having the same method of election for both Houses is that it would tend to produce a mirror image and devalue the role of the House of Lords as a check. If a different method was employed there could be arguments as to which House better represents the wishes of the people.

The House of Commons

There are 650 MPs elected on a constituency basis by those entitled to vote by virtue of the Representation of the People Acts 1983–2000. All Commonwealth citizens and citizens of the Republic of Ireland are entitled to vote if they are 18, are registered on the parliamentary register for that constituency on the qualifying date, and are not subject to any legal incapacity. Those compulsorily detained under the Mental Health Acts are disqualified as are persons convicted of certain corrupt or illegal practices at elections. Convicted criminals in penal institutions have traditionally been disenfranchised but in *Hirst v UK* (ECHR, 2004) it was held that a blanket ban on all prisoners irrespective of the offence or length of sentence was in breach of the ECHR. The **2000 Act** allows people who have no fixed residence to register by allowing them to make a declaration of local connection.

Elections for the Westminster Parliament are conducted by virtue of the "first past the post system", that is the candidate with the largest number of votes in a constituency is returned. This is, however, currently being reconsidered. A referendum on alternative voting is scheduled for 2011 as part of the coalition Government's plan.

Election systems

"First past the post" (majoritarian system): the candidate with the greatest number of votes in the constituency is returned.

Alternate vote (AV) system: May 2011, a UK referendum will be held on AV system. The proposal is for voters to list preferences, if no candidate achieves a clear majority, second choices will be taken into consideration etc, until a clear winner emerges

Proportional representation: various systems claimed to return a parliament more reflective of the views of the electorate. The Scottish parliament uses a hybrid system: electors vote for an individual MSP and a party. The MSP with the greatest number of votes is returned and the party votes and counted to determine the share of the list MSPs.

Eligibility to sit in the Commons (and indeed Lords) is governed by law. The former disqualification of clergy of the established church from membership of the Commons was removed by the House of Commons (Removal of Disqualification) Act 2001. Hereditary peers, apart from those still sitting in the House of Lords, are now no longer disqualified (**House of Lords Act 1999**).

DEVOLUTION OF GOVERNMENT

The Scotland Act 1998

This Act established a Scottish Parliament in Edinburgh (see *http:// www.scottish.parliament.uk*). There are 129 members, 73 of whom are elected under a simple majority system and the remainder by proportional representation using the additional member system. Section 28 authorises the Parliament to make laws known as Acts of the Scottish Parliament. The Scottish Parliament's legislative competence is however limited by s.29 which reserves certain matters for the Westminster Parliament. These are listed in Sch.5 and include foreign affairs, defence of the realm and many financial and economic matters. Under s.29(2)(d) a provision is outwith the competence of the Parliament if it is incompatible with rights under the ECHR or with Community law (s.57(2) provides likewise for members of the Scottish Executive). The Act does not preclude the Westminster Parliament from continuing to legislate for Scotland.

Money is allocated to Scotland by means of a block grant. Part IV of the Act gives the Parliament a tax-varying power of up to three pence in the pound. Fiscal powers are under debate in 2011.

The Act created a Scottish Executive consisting of a First Minister and Ministers drawn from the Members of the Scottish Parliament. The self-styled "Scottish Government" (*http://www.scotland.gov.uk*) considered holding a referendum on increased devolution of powers and separation.

Government of Wales Act 2006

A National Assembly for Wales was established in 1998 (*http://www. assemblywales.org*) and now the Welsh Assembly Government and regulated by the Government of Wales Act 2006 (see *http://wales.gov.uk*). As with the Scottish Parliament, the members are elected by a mixed system; 40 members on a first-past-the-post constituency basis and a further 20 elected using the additional member form of proportional representation. The Assembly delegates executive power to the Welsh Assembly Government consisting of nine cabinet ministers including a First Minister who is nominated by the Assembly and then appointed by the Queen. Its main areas of responsibility are education, enterprise, environment, health and social services, finance, local government and public services, culture, Welsh language and sport, social justice and regeneration. Section 94 of the **2006 Act** has given it devolved power to legislate on such matters as health, education and local government by way of Assembly Measures (s.93). These must be authorised either by specific Acts of Parliament or by legislative competence orders under s.95.

The Northern Ireland Act 1998

Following the Good Friday Agreement in 1998 an elected Assembly was established (*http://www.niassembly.gov.uk*) consisting of 108 members elected by means of the single transferable vote system. Section 1 of the Act declares that Northern Ireland in its entirety remains part of the United Kingdom and shall not cease to be so without the consent of a majority of the people of Northern Ireland. The Assembly was given the power to make laws to be known as Acts and the legislative competence of the Assembly was defined in s.5. As with the Scottish Parliament, certain matters are reserved for the Westminster Parliament. These include matters relating to defence and the Crown. Part III of the Act established the posts of First Minister and Deputy First Minister and empowered them to determine, subject to limitations on the overall number, the number of ministerial offices to be held by Northern Ireland ministers and their functions. One aspect of the Belfast agreement was a power sharing arrangement among the major parties.

The Assembly was suspended from midnight on October 14, 2002. The Northern Ireland (St Andrews Agreement) Act 2006 provided for a transitional assembly in preparation for a restoration of the Northern Ireland Assembly. Elections were held in 2007 and the Assembly was restored on May 8, 2007.

THE WORK OF PARLIAMENT

The passage of legislation

Origins of legislation

At the beginning of each parliamentary session, the Monarch opens Parliament with a speech which outlines the Government's main proposals for the session. Nowadays, the Government tends to intimate in advance the key legislative goals of the forthcoming session. Thus the present coalition cabinet had to thrash out details of primary legislation during early negotiations to ensure both parties managed to secure Parliamentary time for their priority legislative initiatives.

Many Bills undergo a pre-legislative stage, including discussions with interest groups and even wider consultations by green or white papers. Responsibility for drafting the Bill lies with the Parliamentary Draftsmen, officially known as Parliamentary Counsel to the Treasury. Their draft is scrutinised by the Legislation Committee of the Cabinet. The Law Officers are also likely to examine the Bill to consider such matters as the proper legal wording and the practicalities of implementation.

Figure 4.2: Legislative process

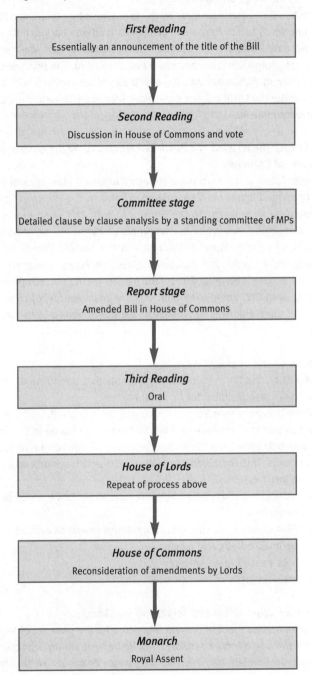

First Reading
Essentially an announcement of the title of the Bill

Second Reading
Discussion in House of Commons and vote

Committee stage
Detailed clause by clause analysis by a standing committee of MPs

Report stage
Amended Bill in House of Commons

Third Reading
Oral

House of Lords
Repeat of process above

House of Commons
Reconsideration of amendments by Lords

Monarch
Royal Assent

The Joint Committee on Human Rights

Every public Bill is now examined by the Joint Committee on Human Rights to determine whether it is convention compliant. It reports back to both Houses. The Government must, by the second reading stage, indicate whether the Bill is or is not compatible with the convention (s.19 HRA). The **HRA** does not, of course, prevent Parliament passing legislation which conflicts with our obligations under the ECHR but any non-compliance must be clearly indicated by the relevant minister.

Procedure for the passing of a Public Bill introduced by the Government into the House of Commons

Most Bills follow a standard track through Parliament (see fig. 4.2).

Once the Bill has been considered in detail by the House of Commons, and approved, it proceeds to the House of Lords. The same process is, in essence, repeated. Any amendments proposed by the House of Lords must be approved by the House of Commons. If the Houses cannot agree, the Commons may invoke the **Parliament Acts 1911/1949** which enable the Commons to pass legislation without the agreement of the Lords (see *Jackson & Others, HMA* (HL, 2005)). The final stage of enactment is, of course, royal assent. All three elements of Parliament are thus involved in the legislative process.

Variations on the Standard Procedure

- Bills may start life in either House but note that the House of Commons has sole responsibility for financial matters.
- Some Bills have their Second Reading Stage in Committee. If the Second Reading is in Committee, the Report Stage will also be in Committee.
- Some Bills have their Committee Stage on the floor of the House in the Commons. This combined committee and report stage procedure can be used for:
  - non-controversial Bills where the Committee Stage would be purely formal;
  - Bills of major constitutional importance where all members wish to be involved at every stage;
  - Bills passed in an emergency;
  - major clauses of Finance Bills.

Effectiveness of parliamentary scrutiny of legislation

It has been argued that the present procedure for the passage of legislation does not provide effective scrutiny, that Parliament simply legitimises that which the Government has decreed. This poses problems for separation of powers.

Effectiveness of Parliamentary Scrutiny of Legislation

Points indicating effective scrutiny	Points indicating less effective scrutiny
Backbench revolts are possible thus Government may need to make concessions	Government usually has a majority and can push measures through by the "whip system"
Bills are open to public scrutiny through the public debates on the floor of the Houses	Government controls the legislative timetable
House of Lords can delay Bills—this can be a powerful tool	House of Lords power limited by the **Parliament Acts 1911/49**
Many amendments can be made and concessions secured through the process of scrutiny	Opposition may oppose Bill as a policy matter rather than a genuine objection to the content
Expert input possible, especially at committee stage	MPs and some Lords may not have expertise on the subject matter

Private Members' Bills

Backbenchers can introduce Bills by being successful in the Ballot, under the 10-Minute Rule or under Standing Order 57.

On average 10–12 Private Members' Bills become law each session. These are mainly Ballot Bills.

Ballot Bills

At a ballot at the beginning of each session, 20 names are drawn out of the hat by the Deputy Speaker. Those members, in order, have an opportunity to introduce their Bills before the House. Six Fridays are set aside in each session for the passage of such Bills although the Government can give extra time to measures it supports to ensure success.

The subjects chosen are wide ranging. A number of important social reforms have resulted from Ballot Bills such as abortion and divorce law reform. The only restriction is that the main purpose of the Bill must not be public expenditure. The procedure is identical to that of any other public Bill. Responsibility for drafting the Bill is borne by the member, although drafting assistance is given to any member whose Bill appears to have a chance of becoming law.

10-Minute-Rule Bills

One member, selected by the Speaker, has ten minutes in which to outline his proposal for legislation. One speech in reply is permitted and the question is then put. The main purpose of this procedure is not to initiate legislation but to generate publicity for a particular issue or to test the water to see if there is support for legislation in the future.

Standing Order 57

Under Standing Order 57, a member may present a Bill without obtaining leave from the House. This allows a member to take advantage of any gap in the Parliamentary timetable (these are rare) and present a measure.

Delegated legislation

Not all legislation is made directly by Parliament. Government ministers, local authorities and other public bodies have been given the power by statute to make subordinate legislation. This may be in the form of statutory instruments and orders, byelaws, regulations and orders in council.

The most important type of delegated legislation made by a minister is a statutory instrument. This is defined and regulated by the Statutory Instruments Act 1946. Delegated legislation made by a minister acting under statutory authority which does not fall within this definition is known as a statutory order. There is no more precise definition as it is simply a residual category. Statutory orders are not regulated by the **1946 Act**.

Delegated legislation

Delegated legislation is used mainly to add detail to primary legislation. It arguably frees up parliamentary time, allowing Parliament to concentrate on the "bigger picture", leaving the details to be worked out elsewhere; facilitates speedy updating of legislation; and allows for technically detailed legislation to be carefully pre-planned in consultation with experts.

It can also be said that the use of delegated legislation is desirable as it allows a certain flexibility in the law enabling a minister, for example, to bring sections of an Act into effect as and when required. But it does have its dangers, particularly when used to effect changes of substance. Then it can be argued that too much power is being concentrated in the hands of the minister. The procedure is much less public than that for the passage of Acts of Parliament. Clearly it is essential that, to prevent abuse, there is adequate control.

Control over delegated legislation

The Enabling Act

The law-making power which Parliament intends to delegate should be expressed in clear and unambiguous language. The grant of wide discretionary powers makes it much more difficult to control the exercise of these powers by means of the doctrine of ultra vires (see Ch.7). Greater control will be achieved by providing that the power is to be exercised by way of statutory instrument. It will then be regulated by the **Statutory Instruments Act 1946** and will, if laid before Parliament, be subject to the scrutiny of the Joint Committee on Delegated Legislation.

Laying before Parliament

The enabling Act can provide that the instrument is to be laid before either or both Houses of Parliament. Various types of laying procedures are used:

- Greatest control is achieved by making the order subject to an affirmative resolution. Parliament must approve the instrument.
- Where an order is subject to a negative resolution, it must be laid before Parliament (usually for 40 days) during which time a member can move a prayer to annul it. The Government can reintroduce the measure, as an order cannot be amended, simply withdrawn.
- Other forms of laying procedure are laying for information only and laying in draft. Section 4 of the **Statutory Instruments Act 1946** says that where a statutory instrument is required to be laid before Parliament then it shall be laid before the instrument comes into operation.

In *R. v Sheer Metalcraft* (HC, 1954) Streatfield J. said that a statutory instrument was complete "when made and laid". Together with s.4 this suggests that laying is a mandatory procedural requirement. However, *R. v Secretary of State for the Environment, Ex p. Leicester CC* (HC, 1985) said that where an order had to be laid before Parliament, laying before the House of Commons was sufficient as there had been substantial compliance with the procedural requirements.

Publication

One difficulty in ensuring adequate scrutiny of delegated legislation is that not all delegated legislation need be published. In the case of statutory orders, any specific requirements as to publication must be stated in the enabling Act. Most statutory instruments must be sent to the Queen's Printer, numbered and put on sale (s.2). Failure to comply with s.2 does not render the order invalid (*Sheer Metalcraft*, above).

It should, however, be noted, that s.3(2) of the Act provides a limited defence in the case of a person charged with an offence under an unpublished statutory instrument. In any proceedings it shall be a defence for the accused to prove that, at the date of the alleged contravention, the instrument had not been published. It is then up to the minister to defeat the defence by proving that he had taken reasonable steps to bring the purport of the instrument to the notice of the public or of persons likely to be affected by it, or of the person charged. It is unlikely that this defence will be available in the case of every unpublished statutory instrument. The wording of s.3(2) appears to confine it to instruments which should have been published but, in fact, were not.

Scrutiny by Parliamentary Committee

The Joint Committee on Statutory Instruments, which comprises seven members from each House plus a chairman drawn from the Opposition benches in the Commons, can examine all general statutory instruments and all other statutory orders subject to the affirmative procedure or special procedure orders. It is not concerned with the merits of the instruments but rather with whether the special attention of the House should be drawn to the legislation. The Committee can consider only a fraction of the instruments laid before Parliament. Even when the Committee draws special attention to an instrument, no special Parliamentary notice need be taken. Indeed, by the time the Committee has reported, the instrument in question may have been dealt with.

Scrutiny by the courts

The courts may be asked to consider whether delegated legislation is ultra vires the enabling Act (see Ch.7). In interpreting the width of the power to make delegated legislation, the courts will apply certain presumptions, e.g. that there is no power to impose a tax unless stated expressly (*Att-Gen v Wilts United Dairies* (CA, 1921)); that there is no power to oust the citizen's right of access to the courts (*Chester v Bateson* (HC, 1920)); that the regulation will not operate retrospectively.

PARLIAMENTARY SCRUTINY OF THE EXECUTIVE

Not since the nineteenth century can it be said that Parliament has made policy directly. This function has long since passed to the Cabinet. Parliament can still influence policy-making, acting during its formulation by way of various interest groups and committees and by general expression of opinion on the floor of the House. After all, constitutionally, ministers are answerable to Parliament for the conduct of their departments. Parliamentary scrutiny of the executive is an important aspect of the checks and balances inherent in separation of powers (see Ch.2).

Parliamentary scrutiny
Under the doctrine of separation of powers, Parliament has an important role to play in scrutinising the Executive, to ensure no arbitrary abuse of power.
Debates—on the floor of the Houses of Parliament.
Parliamentary questions—written or oral questions to a Minister of State.
Select committees—detailed consideration of policy/law by backbench MPs and Lords.

Debates

The Opposition parties have 20 days in each session in which they can select the topic for debate. The Government itself provides time to debate such matters as the armed services and the EU. Emergency debates are allowed at the discretion of the Speaker under Standing Order 24 if he considers that an application relates to "a specific and important matter that should have urgent consideration". The application must be supported by 40 members.

Certain opportunities are given to backbenchers to choose the subject matter for debate. Examples are:

- adjournment debates—half-hour debates at the end of each day's sitting. Members ballot for a right to choose a topic and speak. A government minister will reply;
- ten Fridays and four half days are given for private members' motions;
- adjournment debates following the passage of the Consolidated Fund and Appropriation Bills.

Apart from emergency debates which, because of their rarity, will command widespread coverage in the media, such debates have limited value.

Since 1999 debates have also been held in Westminster Hall. These have tended to deal with constituency matters and other issues such as select committee reports which would be unlikely to be debated in the main House because of lack of time.

Parliamentary questions

There are written and oral questions.

Oral questions

Ministers are questioned in the House on a rota basis for 45 to 55 minutes on Mondays to Thursdays. The Prime Minister now only faces questions once a week on Wednesdays. Members give at least three days' notice of a question and the questions are listed in the order in which they are tabled.

According to Erskine May the purpose of questions is to obtain information, to press for action. It now appears that question time is used mostly for the following purposes:

- to embarrass the Government by raising a sensitive issue;
- to publicise a particular matter, either nationally or in the MP's own constituency;
- to keep the minister on his toes, to ensure he is *au fait* with the activities of his department;
- some questions asked by the Government's own backbenchers are "planted" by the minister to enable him to release information;
- Prime Minister's question time is often used by the Opposition to make political points.

Question time has limited use in obtaining the factual information necessary to enable MPs to scrutinise the activities of the Government. Ministers have warning of questions and need disclose no more information than they think fit and are obliged only to answer those matters which fall within their particular areas of responsibility. Thus as a formal method of scrutiny it has little value.

Written answers to questions

Questions not dealt with on the floor of the House are answered in writing by the minister and the answers published in *Hansard*. In addition, questions may be put down for written answer. Such questions are designed to obtain factual information and/or to take up matters on behalf of constituents.

Although these may produce useful information, ministers are skilled in revealing no more than is necessary. One basic defect in these methods of scrutiny is that MPs must know the right questions to ask. As government becomes more complex, it becomes increasingly difficult for MPs to have sufficient specialist knowledge to identify the key areas for investigation. Specialist knowledge, developed through membership of parliamentary committees, has proved invaluable here.

Parliamentary select committees

A more effective method of scrutiny than can be employed on the floor of the House is scrutiny by committees of MPs. Fourteen departmental select committees were established in 1979 to shadow the various departments of state. The number has increased considerably since then but they still reflect upon government departments. Some committees, such as EU, now have appointed sub-committees. The House of Lords has fewer select committees, each with a broader range of expertise represented. In addition, there are joint (between the Lords and Commons) select committees, the most prominent (and permanent) of which are on human rights and on statutory instruments.

Membership
Committees normally consist of 11 MPs, their membership reflecting party balance in the House. The chairmanships are shared between the main parties, the Government traditionally retaining some of the most sensitive, e.g. Defence, for itself. The committee members are appointed by the Committee of Selection. There is keen competition among backbenchers for places on the most prestigious committees and some complaints that the Committee of Selection, which is essentially controlled by the party whips, tends to appoint mainstream party members to the exclusion of perhaps more formidable establishment critics.

Select Committees

Select committees should "provide continuous and systematic scrutiny of the activities of the public service and to base that scrutiny on the subject areas within the responsibility of the individual Government Departments". They thus:

- examine departmental estimates, the policy objectives underlying these and consider whether the expenditure incurred would achieve these objectives in an economical manner;
- examine all aspects of administration and policy relating to the department;
- undertake special studies of areas of importance within the ambit of the department;
- examine delegated legislation and European secondary legislation;
- monitor departmental performance against a host of targets.

Powers
The committees are empowered to take evidence from ministers, civil servants and outside experts and to call for the necessary papers and records. They will question regulators and the chairs of the various executive agencies. The committee must, however, rely on Parliament to enforce these powers and this depends on the wishes of the Government of the day. The

1988 report, *Improving Management in Government, the Next Steps*, led to the establishment of a number of government agencies. The aim was to rationalise the bureaucracy and to introduce a more management-oriented system. These agencies now carry out many of the functions formerly performed by the various government departments. Operational matters are made the responsibility of the chief executive of each agency which is run by a management board. The Permanent Secretary to the Department carries out a monitoring function on behalf of the Secretary of State. The Permanent Secretary remains the principal adviser on policy matters.

Assessment
The committees have produced a considerable amount of valuable information which must assist MPs in their general task of scrutiny. In general it can be argued that investigations into specific problems have been more valuable than wide ranging background investigations.

Where a committee can issue a quick and reasoned comment on a topical subject it has the greatest impact. Committees are beginning to time their reports to correspond with appropriate business, such as legislation or a planned debate, and this ensures greater coverage of their report.

A major problem has been the delay before the government department in question produces any response to the report. There have been no problems in staffing the committees and the membership has remained relatively static. This has enabled MPs to build up considerable expertise in their chosen fields. The committees have all appointed specialist advisers. There is some evidence that committee members feel themselves less fettered by party ties in committee than on the floor of the House although there has been a tendency for party loyalty to reassert itself if the report is debated. Many reports are debated in Westminster Hall.

Yet the committees cannot force ministers and civil servants to divulge information. The Government has made it clear that it believes a civil servant's responsibility is to his minister, not to Parliament. Recent reports on the evidential basis of the invasion of Iraq (now subject to the Chilcot inquiry) and the Hutton review have raised public concerns on the effectiveness of scrutiny of sensitive matters.

Although select committees offer a clear opportunity for scrutiny, there is little evidence to support the view that the committees exercise any real systematic control over the activities of government.

Control over financial matters
Constitutionally, Parliament has control over taxation and expenditure, although once again decisions are made by the Government. In recent years the Chancellor of the Exchequer has combined his statement on public

expenditure with his Budget speech. Those taxes imposed annually must be authorised by the **Finance Act**. Authority for levying taxation in the interim period is given by the Provisional Collection of Taxes Act 1968, a resolution of the House of Commons being insufficient authority (*Bowles v The Bank of England* (HC, 1913)).

Parliament's contribution to this process is confined to debates on the Budget and formal approval of government spending (e.g. by passing **Consolidated Fund Acts** and **Annual Appropriation Acts** which authorise payments out of the consolidated fund and the **Finance Act** which implements the Government's tax proposals). There is little detailed Parliamentary control and no Parliamentary control over government borrowing.

The Comptroller and Auditor General, appointed by the Crown on a resolution of the House of Commons by virtue of s.1(1) of the **National Audit Act 1983**, has two major functions:

- to ensure that all money paid out of the government accounts has been properly authorised and is properly applied; and
- to examine the accounts of the various government departments.

Under the **Audit Act 1983** this is more than a traditional audit. S/he is entitled to consider whether "objectives have been achieved in the most economical way". This has become known as "value for money" and "efficiency" auditing. The National Audit Office (*http://www.nao.org.uk*), of which s/he is head, is also responsible for auditing the accounts of a wide range of bodies dependent on funds from Central Government.

. . . .

PARLIAMENTARY PRIVILEGE

To ensure that Members of Parliament and Parliament as a whole can carry out their functions effectively, they have certain privileges to safeguard them from outside interference.

Privilege of freedom of speech

To ensure an MP is free to carry out his parliamentary duties and speak freely without fear of any legal repercussions, an MP has the privilege of free speech.

Absolute privilege

MPs have absolute privilege with regard to words spoken in the course of parliamentary proceedings (**The Bill of Rights** Art.9). Not only does this protect against actions of defamation but also against any criminal charges. Nor can they be found to be in contempt of court in relation to words spoken in the course of proceedings in Parliament. Perhaps the most serious incident was where several MPs deliberately identified an officer of the security services who had given evidence in court under the name Colonel B. The court had warned that any attempt to name the officer would be a contempt of court. No action could be taken by the court against the MPs.

In *Church of Scientology v Johnson Smith* (HC, 1972) an attempt was made to sue an MP claiming that he had slandered the Church of Scientology and its members. In order to succeed, it was necessary to show that the MP had spoken with malice. It was attempted to prove this by relying on a speech made by him in Parliament. The court held that these words could not be used as the words were absolutely privileged.

What are "proceedings before Parliament"?

It clearly covers debates, questions and everything said and done by a member both in committee and on the floor of the House. But as Erskine May points out, it does not follow that everything which is said and done within the confines of the chamber during a debate or other business forms part of a proceeding in Parliament. It would not, for example, cover a private conversation between two MPs. Nor does the geographical location of the speaker give automatic protection: *Rivlin v Bilainkin* (HC, 1953).

DEFINITION CHECKPOINT

"Proceedings before Parliament"

A former Select Committee on Privileges recommended that the term "proceedings before Parliament" should cover:

- all things done or written in each House or in Committee for the purpose of business being transacted;
- all things done between members and officers, between members, and between members and ministers for the purpose of enabling any of these to carry out their functions.

A possible limitation to this is the suggestion that it would cover only those matters which had been before the House, or at least those coming before the House in the current parliamentary session (see *Rost v Edwards* (HC, 1990)).

Qualified privilege

An MP may rely on the defence of qualified privilege in regard to words spoken in the course of his duty as an MP. This means that he is protected against any action of defamation provided he speaks in good faith and without malice (*Beach v Freeson* (HC, 1972)), and provided there is a common interest between the parties.

Following the case of *Prebble v Television New Zealand Ltd* (PC, 1995), the High Court halted a libel action by Neil Hamilton MP against the Guardian newspaper on the basis that much of the evidence could not be explored as it related to "proceedings in Parliament". The potential unfairness of this led Parliament to amend Art.9 of the **Bill of Rights**. The Defamation Act 1996 allows individuals to waive the rule which prevents evidence of proceedings in Parliament being considered by a court.

Reports of parliamentary proceedings

At common law, no protection was given to those reporting speeches made in Parliament. The MP was absolutely privileged but the reporter and the publisher could face civil or criminal action (*Stockdale v Hansard* (HL, 1839), where libel damages were awarded against *Hansard* who had printed verbatim an authorised House of Commons Report).

Protection is now given by the Parliamentary Papers Act 1840. Section 1 gives absolute protection against any civil or criminal action to anyone publishing papers printed by order of Parliament. This will cover, for example, White Papers and *Hansard*, the daily journal of the House. Section 2 gives absolute protection to any copy of such paper. Section 3 only protects against actions of defamation in that it gives qualified privilege to extracts from any reports protected by ss.1 and 2. This means that such extracts are protected provided the defendant can show that they were published in good faith and without malice (*Dingle v Associated Newspapers* (HC, 1960)). No special protection has been given to the broadcasting of the proceedings of the House but broadcasters can claim the protection given to any fair and accurate report under the **1996 Act**.

Privilege of freedom from arrest

MPs have no privilege protecting them against an arrest on criminal charges but they are protected against arrest in connection with a civil matter while Parliament is in session and for 40 days before and after. The arrest of MPs following the expenses scandal in 2009–2010 demonstrates the limit of this privilege.

Parliament's right to regulate its own internal proceedings

Parliament is empowered to regulate its own internal proceedings. It may make standing orders to govern its procedures. The courts have always refused to consider whether these procedures have been complied with (*Pickin v British Rail Board* (HL, 1974)).

The privilege is much wider than procedural matters, covering every aspect of the internal functions of the House. In *R. v Graham-Campbell, Ex p.*

Herbert (HC, 1935) the court refused to investigate an alleged breach of the licensing laws by the "Kitchen Committee" of the House of Commons.

In *Bradlaugh v Gossett* (HC, 1884), Parliament expelled an MP who refused to take the oath of allegiance to the Crown under the Parliamentary Oaths Act 1866, on the grounds that he was an atheist and the oath would be meaningless. At a by-election he was re-elected and indicated that he was now willing to take the requisite oath. Parliament resolved that he should be prevented, if necessary by force, from taking his seat. The court would not intervene.

Parliament's power to punish for contempt
The following have been held to be contempts of Parliament:
- an attempt to interfere with a member's freedom of action (*NUPE case* (HC, 1976/77));
- misconduct in the House or disobedience of the rules of the House, e.g. failure to co-operate with a Parliamentary Committee, disruptive behaviour in the House;
- misconduct by MPs in the House. Corruption, taking bribes, failure to declare a conflict in interests have all constituted contempts. Recent concerns have related to the employment of MPs as consultants and lobbyists and the employment of ex-cabinet ministers in positions where use could be made of their "inside knowledge" (see the Nolan Report);
- publication of materials reflecting on the proceedings of the House and its members. Newspaper articles criticising MPs have been held to be a contempt (*Sunday People Case* (HC, 1976/7)).

Thus contempt is wider than simply a breach of any of Parliament's privileges but can consist of any conduct which interferes with the workings of Parliament or is likely to bring Parliament or its members into disrepute. Members can be suspended or expelled for contempt. The House also has the power to admonish or issue a reprimand to those in contempt.

Members' financial interests
Following the Poulson scandal in the early 1970s where three MPs had misused their position as MPs to promote Poulson's business interests, the House set up a register of members' interests to make public any business and other interests which might influence their behaviour. A number of incidents in the early 1990s culminating in the "cash for questions" affair led to the establishment of the Nolan Committee into Standards in Public Life. This, in turn, led to the establishment of the Parliamentary Commissioner for Standards, a much more comprehensive register of members' interests, a

reformed Committee of Standards and Privileges and a standing committee to inquire into standards in public life. This latter committee has considered, for example, the relationship between MPs and lobbyists. The Parliamentary Commissioner for Standards has carried out well over a hundred investigations into the activities of MPs, including alleged failure to register notifiable interests. The courts have refused to review the Commissioner's activities as they are concerned with matters within Parliament (*R. v Commissioner for Standards, Ex p. Al-Fayed* (CA, 1998)).

Revision checklist

You should now know and understand:

- the composition of Parliament;
- the legislative process;
- the powers of Parliament to scrutinise the executive;
- the impact of parliamentary privilege.

QUESTION AND ANSWER

Question

"The Westminster Parliament is no longer at the heart of the political and government processes in the United Kingdom and plays an ever-decreasing role in calling the Government to account."

Discuss.

Advice and the Answer

This is a basic essay question on the extent to which Parliament can truly be said to hold the executive (government) to account. It overlaps slightly with aspects discussed in the question at the end of Ch.3 (separation of powers). An answer would be expected to demonstrate an understanding of the role of Parliament and the opportunities it has to call the Government to account, drawing on the material on parliamentary scrutiny. It is feasible to briefly discuss the importance of Parliament calling the Government to account from the standpoint of separation of powers and the needs for adequate checks and balances on the exercise of power.

1. Key opportunities for scrutiny

Legislation may be considered but note it is not always a part of constitutional and administrative law courses (being studied under English Legal Systems). Irrespective of legislative scrutiny being examined, consideration should be given to debates, parliamentary select committees and questions.

2. Limitations on parliamentary scrutiny—external factors

Consideration of the factors which have restricted the central role of the Westminster Parliament:

- influence of the EU;
- devolution;
- changes in the House of Lords which have limited its credibility;
- increased tendency to announce policy outside the House;
- Government control over Parliament through whip system, patronage, control of timetable, etc.—possibly strengthened as a result of the modernisation changes.

Although it should be noted that in formal legal terms, Parliament still provides the Government and must approve legislation, grant of supply and taxation.

3. A diminishing power of Parliament to scrutinise executive?

Consider whether Parliament's role in calling the Government to account has diminished. Consider:

(a) Practical significance of ministerial responsibility—minister's response to criticism-naming and blaming civil servants; sheltering behind chief executives of next step agencies; the lack of relationship between fault and resignation.

(b) Effectiveness of questioning ministers—the use of written and oral questions—the ability to avoid answering; government control over information; the use of Prime Minister's question time; question time used for other purposes.

(c) Traditional opportunities for scrutiny and their limitations; the Government majority, the Whip system and control of the timetable; lack of publicity, e.g. adjournment debates.

(d) Effectiveness of select committees—more effective scrutiny because of specialist knowledge, ability to call witnesses, select topic, production of information, etc. Note, however, the reliance on Parliament to compel attendance; particular problem in obtaining answers from civil servants who are accountable to their minister; no systematic scrutiny of expenditure.

4. Conclusion

It may be useful to note in conclusion that effective scrutiny depends on knowing the questions to ask and having access to relevant information—reference could be made to Parliamentary Resolutions on openness and accountability and questions and procedures for ministers regarding duty of disclosure to the House. This is a good example when your awareness of current affairs can be demonstrated. There are always a number of good examples of the Government and its Ministers being held to account and/or avoiding being held to account—keep a note of these over the duration of your course.

The Police and the Public

5

INTRODUCTION

In this chapter we will look at the following powers of the police:

- stop and search;
- arrest;
- detention and questioning at the police station;
- entry, search and seizure.

These powers are essential for the police to fulfil their duties of preventing and detecting crime. The police are entrusted with the power to investigate offences, yet, just because a person comes under suspicion of being involved in criminal activity, this does not mean that he loses all rights to the freedom of his person. The law has to strike a balance between preserving and safeguarding the rights of individuals and giving the police the necessary powers to carry out these tasks effectively. In this chapter we will look at the powers given to the police and the safeguards that are incorporated into those powers to strike this balance and prevent them being used arbitrarily.

THE INVESTIGATION OF OFFENCES

Section 6 of the **Human Rights Act 1998** makes it unlawful for the police, as a public authority, to act in a way that is incompatible with a convention right. Thus the police, in investigating offences will, for example, have to act in accordance with Arts 5, 6 and 8 of the ECHR. Any restrictions on an individual's liberty must be framed with sufficient precision to allow the citizen to foresee the consequences of their actions and avoid the grant of arbitrary power.

The police have the right to ask anyone questions in the course of their duties but, although there may be a moral duty to help the police, there is no legal duty.

(a) There is no obligation to answer questions (*Rice v Connolly* (HL, 1966)). A person should not be forced to incriminate himself. It should be noted that, although a suspect is still able to choose to remain silent, in certain circumstances a failure to answer questions might have evidential consequences. Under s.34 of the Criminal Justice and Public Order Act 1994 where a suspect is being questioned under caution or is being charged with an offence, and fails to mention a fact which he subsequently relies on in his defence, the court may be allowed to draw an adverse inference from the suspect's silence, if it considers it to have been reasonable for the accused to have mentioned the fact when questioned or charged.

Under s.36, a similar inference may be drawn from a failure to provide an explanation where objects, substances or marks are found on a suspect or in the place the suspect was at the time of the offence. Before such an inference can be drawn, the requirements of s.36(b), (c) and (d) must be satisfied (see *R. v Argent* (CA, 1996)).

Silence on its own will not, of itself, be sufficient evidence of guilt. The prosecution will always be required to produce other evidence.

(b) Failure to answer police questions does not, by itself, amount to obstruction of the police in the execution of their duty.

(c) If a person is voluntarily helping the police, that person is entitled to terminate the interview and leave at any time. If the police wish to detain him they must place him under arrest. Section 29 of the Police and Criminal Evidence Act 1984 (PACE) provides that he should be informed at once that he is under arrest if a decision is taken to prevent him leaving at will.

. . . .

STOP AND SEARCH

In the course of their duties the police may wish to search a suspect for evidence of an offence. This power has long been seen as a contentious area of police activity and a major cause of tension between minority groups and the police. The Stephen Lawrence Inquiry highlighted its negative effect on community relations and led to the Code of Practice on Stop and Search (Code A) being revised in an attempt to provide greater safeguards against any discriminatory use of the power. The **PACE** Codes of Practice supplement the Act itself and give guidance upon the powers and responsibilities of the police.

Code A emphasises that the power must be used fairly and responsibly with respect for people being searched and without unlawful discrimination.

A police officer can only carry out a stop and search where there is a legal power to do so. The consent of the suspect is no longer enough. The only exception to this is where a search is carried out as a condition of entry, e.g. to sports events.

Who can be stopped and searched?

Under s.1 of **PACE** the police can stop and search:

(a) any person or vehicle;

(b) anything which is in or on a vehicle,

What can the police look for?

Section 1 states the police can only stop and search in order to look for stolen or prohibited articles, fireworks or articles with blades or points as defined in s.139 of the **Criminal Justice Act 1988,** and may detain a person or vehicle in order to conduct such a search. Section 1(6) gives the power to seize such items. A prohibited article includes:

(a) an offensive weapon;

(b) an article made for, or intended to be used for, burglary, theft, theft of a motor vehicle, obtaining property by deception or destroying or damaging property.

When can a stop and search be carried out?

The officer must have reasonable grounds to suspect that that the person they want to search has on their person/vehicle such stolen or prohibited articles etc (s.1(3)). Whether such grounds exist will depend on the circumstances of each case but there must be some objective basis for it. Code of Practice A on stop and search says that an officer will need to consider the nature of the article suspected of being carried in the context of other factors such as the time, place and behaviour of the person concerned or those with him. Reasonable suspicion may exist, for example, when information has been received such as a description of an article being carried.

What are reasonable grounds?

Reasonable suspicion can never be supported on the basis of personal factors alone. For example a person's colour, age, hairstyle or manner of dress, or the fact that he is known to have a previous conviction for possession of an unlawful article, cannot be used alone or in combination with each other as the sole basis on which to search that person. Nor may suspicion be founded on the basis of stereotyped images of certain persons or groups as more likely to be committing offences. Personal factors can, of course, be taken into account together with other, more objective factors. Thus reasonable suspicion should normally be linked to accurate intelligence.

The extent of the search

The Code envisages a minimal interference with a person's liberty. The suspect's co-operation must be sought and every effort made to avoid embarrassment. Under s.117 of **PACE** reasonable force may be used if necessary. Searches are restricted to superficial examination of outer clothing. Section 60AA of the **Criminal Justice and Public Order Act 1994** allows the police to remove items such as masks which are being used to conceal the suspect's identity and the **Terrorism Act 2000** does permit the removal of headgear and footwear in public when conducting a search under that Act. The thoroughness and extent of the search depends on what is suspected of being carried. So, for example, if the suspicion relates to an article slipped into a pocket, the power of search will relate only to that pocket. If a fuller search is deemed necessary, it must be done in a suitable place by an officer of the same sex and, unless the suspect consents to accompany the officer, he must first be arrested. As was noted above, in certain circumstances a failure to answer questions may have evidential consequences.

Location of search

The power can be exercised in any place to which the public has access whether on payment or not, excluding dwelling houses or other private premises such as private clubs. It covers streets, common areas of flats, such as stairs and walkways, pub car parks, etc. Note, however, the position relating to the yards and gardens of houses. The police cannot use stop and search powers there unless they are satisfied that the suspect does not reside there, or is there without the permission of the owner of the property (ss.1(4) and 1(5)).

Other powers

PACE does not encompass all existing stop and search powers. Other powers are given by such Acts as the Misuse of Drugs Act 1971 (permits the police to stop and search for controlled drugs anywhere). Under s.60 of the **Criminal Justice and Public Order Act 1994** (CJPOA), where it is reasonably believed that incidents involving serious violence may take place in a locality and it is expedient to use the powers given under the Act to prevent their occurrence, an officer of the rank of Inspector or above may authorise special stop and search powers (see Ch.5). A uniformed officer may then search any person for offensive weapons. The police also have powers under s.43 **Terrorism Act 2000** to stop and search individuals whom they reasonably suspect to be a terrorist. The power under s.44 **Terrorism Act 2000** whereby an officer of the rank of Assistant Chief Constable or above could authorise stop and search powers in a specified locality for up to 28 days if they considered it expedient for the prevention of acts of terrorism was amended in July 2010. One of the factors involved in amending the law was the decision of the European Court of Human Rights (ECtHR) in the case of *Gillan and Quinton v UK* (Jan 2010, final decision June 2010). As with s.60 **CJPOA** there was no need for the officer making the stop to have any level of suspicion against the person being stopped. The ECtHR ruled that such a power did not contain sufficient safeguards for members of the public against potential arbitrary abuse and as such it violated art.8 of the ECHR. The Home Secretary issued guidelines on July 8, 2010 to the police upon the use of s.44. She removed the ability to carry out such searches without reasonable suspicion. She also declared that s.44 can only be used in relation to vehicles. Any searches for individuals must be made using s.43 powers. These guidelines are interim measures only. A full review of all counter terrorism legislation will be undertaken by the new Government.

Safeguards

As well as the requirement for the officer to have reasonable grounds to conduct a stop and search, there are additional safeguards. Before a search takes place the officer must comply with the requirements of s.2 **PACE**. These include the following:

(a) the officer must identify himself (s.2(3)(a)). Failure to do so will invalidate the search and make it unlawful (*Osman v DPP* (HC, 1999));

(b) he must take reasonable steps to explain what he is looking for and the basis of his suspicion (s.2(3)(b)).

After the search

(a) He must normally make a record of the search there and then unless there are exceptional circumstances. This record should cover the ethnic group, identity of the suspect, object, grounds of search, place and time, date and results (s.3). This record should be made available to the suspect on request and is designed to facilitate any complaints of unjustifiable action by the police.

(b) If an unattended vehicle has been searched, a note should be left recording this fact and indicating the officer responsible (s.2(6)).

These requirements have become more stringent over the years and now apply to all searches.

Figure 5.1: Stop and search summary

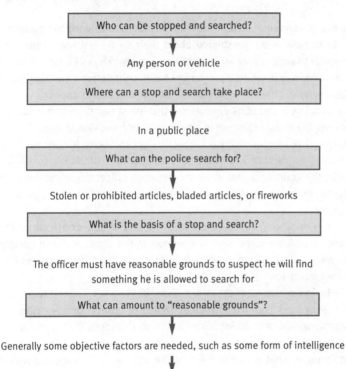

Who can be stopped and searched?

↓

Any person or vehicle

Where can a stop and search take place?

↓

In a public place

What can the police search for?

↓

Stolen or prohibited articles, bladed articles, or fireworks

What is the basis of a stop and search?

↓

The officer must have reasonable grounds to suspect he will find something he is allowed to search for

What can amount to "reasonable grounds"?

↓

Generally some objective factors are needed, such as some form of intelligence

↓

Personal factors alone cannot usually amount to reasonable grounds

↓

Sometimes, behaviour alone can give rise to sufficient reasonable grounds

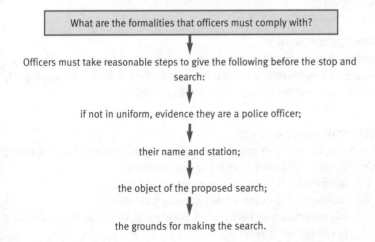

What are the formalities that officers must comply with?

↓

Officers must take reasonable steps to give the following before the stop and search:

↓

if not in uniform, evidence they are a police officer;

↓

their name and station;

↓

the object of the proposed search;

↓

the grounds for making the search.

ARREST

This is a fundamental step in the criminal process designed to ensure that a person is able to be questioned about their suspected involvement in an offence or to ensure they are available to answer charges before a court. It is not the only way in which a person can be brought before a court. In the case of less serious offences a person can be summonsed to appear.

Article 5 of the ECHR emphasises that arrest and detention must not be arbitrary. The reasonableness of a police officer's decision to arrest has to be considered bearing in mind a suspect's right to liberty (*Cummings v Chief Constable of Northumbria Police* (CA, 2003)). In *Castorina v CC of Surrey* (1988), the court said that while the arresting officer might not yet be in a position to prove anything, he must have some factual basis for his suspicion.

In *Hough v Chief Constable of Staffordshire* (CA, 2001) the arresting officer's suspicion came from information in the police national computer. This was, in fact, wrong. Despite this the court held that there was "reasonable suspicion".

In *Commissioner of the Police of the Metropolis v Raissi* (CA, 2008) the court examined the circumstances where a police officer relies upon instructions from a superior officer to arrest a suspect. The court confirmed previous decisions that had looked at this issue and stated that the important factor is what is in the mind of the arresting office themselves—they must have the requisite reasonable grounds of suspicion—it is not sufficient to rely upon instructions from another officer, even if they are of superior rank. In this case the arresting officer did rely upon instructions from a superior officer when arresting Raissi, without himself having the requisite reasonable grounds—the arrest was therefore unlawful.

Arrest under warrant

Under s.1 of the Magistrates' Court Act 1980, a warrant for arrest may be issued by a magistrate on sworn information by the police. It must identify the suspect and the offence on which it is founded.

Summary power of arrest

Section 24 as amended by the Serious Organised Crime and Police Act 2005 gives the police a power to arrest without a warrant:

(a) anyone who is about to commit an offence;
(b) anyone who is in the act of committing an offence;
(c) anyone whom they have reasonable grounds for suspecting to be about to commit an offence;

(d) anyone whom they have reasonable grounds for suspecting to be committing an offence.

Where an offence has been committed, or the officer has reasonable grounds to suspect an offence has been committed, he may also arrest anyone he reasonably suspects to be guilty.

In all instances this is subject to the requirement that the arrest is necessary in terms of one of the reasons specified in s.24(5). These include:

(a) where the officer cannot discover the suspect's name or address or believes he has been given a false name or address;
(b) to prevent the person causing physical harm to himself or another; suffering physical injury; causing loss or damage to property; committing an offence against public decency; causing an unlawful obstruction of the highway;
(c) to protect a child;
(d) to allow prompt and effective investigation of the issue;
(e) to prevent any prosecution being hindered by the disappearance of the suspect.

Section 24A allows the ordinary citizen to make an arrest in a more restricted range of circumstances. It relates only to indictable offences. There is no preventative power of arrest nor where it is only suspected that an offence has been committed. Again the person making the arrest must either know or have reasonable grounds to believe the suspect is guilty and must also have reasonable grounds to believe that an arrest is necessary in terms of s.24A(4) and it is not reasonably practicable for a constable to make the arrest instead.

The reasons in s.24A(4) are to prevent a person:

(a) causing physical injury to himself or others;
(b) suffering physical injury;
(c) causing loss of or damage to property;
(d) making off before he can be handed over to a constable.

Formalities of arrest

As we saw with stop and search powers (s.2), for the police to carry out their duties lawfully certain information must be given to individuals. Section 28 sets out the information that must be given to those who are placed under arrest. The section expressly states that a failure to give the required information makes the arrest unlawful.

The Act requires the person arrested to be informed that he is under arrest as soon as practicable even if the fact that he is under arrest is obvious (ss.28(1) and (2)).

He must also be told of the ground of the arrest at the time or as soon as is practicable thereafter (s.28(3) and *DPP v Hawkins* (HC, 1988)). In *Edwards v DPP* (HC, 1993) the fact that the police officer gave a wrong reason for the arrest, rendered the arrest invalid.

Section 28 enacts in statutory form the rule laid down in *Christie v Leachinsky* (HL, 1947) where Lord Simon said that the suspect was entitled to know on what charge or on suspicion of what crime he was seized. If the citizen is not so informed the police may be liable for false imprisonment unless, of course, the suspect makes this impossible by his conduct (*Lewis v Chief Constable of South Wales* (CA, 1990)). Lord Simon stressed that technical or precise language need not be used (see *Abbassy v Newman* (CA, 1989)). Section 28 varies the decision in *Leachinsky* in that Lord Simon said that if the facts were obvious—if, for example, the suspect has been caught red handed—it was not necessary to inform him why he had been arrested. Section 28(4) now says that the person must be told the reason for the arrest even if the facts are obvious (*Nicholas v DPP* (HC, 1987)).

Arrest elsewhere than at a police station

Section 30 says that, on arrest, a suspect should be taken to a police station as soon as practicable unless the investigation requires his presence elsewhere. This must normally be a designated station, that is one which has a custody officer and has the necessary facilities to cope with those detained following arrest. But, see *Vince v Chief Constable of Dorset* (CA, 1992). He need not be taken to a designated police station if it is not anticipated he will be detained for more than six hours or where the arresting officer is without help.

Once the decision is taken to arrest a suspect he must not normally be interviewed about the offence except at a police station. This is to ensure the various protections noted below will apply. An interview is defined in para.11 of Code C.

Search on arrest

Section 32 regulates searches where an arrest is made away from a police station. A constable has a right to search for a weapon if he has reasonable grounds for believing that the suspect might present a danger to himself or others, for example because he was acting violently or was drunk or suicidal. The suspect may also be searched for anything he could use to effect his escape and for evidence relating to any offence if there are reasonable grounds for suspecting that the items are in the suspect's possession.

Such a search must be relatively cursory. If a person is searched in public he cannot be required to remove anything other than his coat, jacket or gloves.

Figure 5.2: Arrest summary

For a lawful arrest there are three aspects which need to be fulfilled:

"Grounds" of arrest must exist

The arresting officer needs "reasonable grounds to suspect" that the person they want to arrest:
- has committed an offence (past); OR
- is in the process of committing an offence (present); OR
- is about to commit an offence (future).

The arrest must be "necessary"

In addition to having grounds of arrest, the arresting officer also needs to be able to show that the arrest is necessary for one of the factors set out below (from s.24(5) **PACE**):
- to obtain the arrestee's name or address where the officer either does not know it, cannot obtain it, or believes the information given is incorrect;
- to prevent the arrestee harming themselves, somebody else, or damaging property;
- to prevent the arrestee from committing an offence against public decency;
- to prevent the arrestee from causing an unlawful obstruction of the high way;
- to protect a child or vulnerable person;
- to allow the prompt and effective investigation of the offence;
- to prevent the person disappearing and hindering the investigation of the offence.

The "formalities" of arrest must be complied with

In addition to the above two aspects, the arrest must be carried out in the correct manner for it to be lawful. This means that the following information must be given to the arrestee (from s.28 **PACE**):
- they must be told they are under arrest as soon as possible, even if it is obvious that they are under arrest;
- the grounds for arrest must be given, even if they are obvious.

Following an arrest the police may search the premises where the suspect was immediately prior to or at the time of the arrest for evidence relating to that offence (s.32(2)(b)); *R. v Beckford* (CA, 1991)). If he has been arrested for an indictable offence, there may also be a power to search his home under s.18 (discussed later).

Section 54 requires the custody officer to ascertain what property a detained person has with him. He is responsible for its safekeeping. To that end he is entitled to search him. Cash and items of value are kept for safekeeping. The detained person can retain his clothing and personal effects unless the custody officer considers that, in terms of s.54(4), he may use them to cause harm to himself or others, effect an escape, damage property or interfere with evidence.

Code C defines personal effects as those items which a person may lawfully need or use etc, not including cash or other items of value (para.4.3).

Anything else can be seized. Intimate and strip searches must be conducted in accordance with Annexe A to Code C.

Under s.54(6)A, there is a power to search a suspect in custody at any time to ascertain whether he has anything he could use for the purposes specified in s.54(4).

Intimate searches are regulated by s.55 and Annexe A of Code C.

QUESTIONING IN POLICE CUSTODY

The opportunity to question suspects in custody is clearly of crucial importance to the police. The suspect, however, is in a very vulnerable situation. The recognition in **PACE** of the power to detain suspects after arrest, but before charge, is balanced by attempts to give some protection to the suspect. These arise from the imposition of maximum time limits for detention, periodic review of the need for such detention, the statutory rights of access to a solicitor and a Code of Practice on Detention and Questioning (Code C). The custody officer has a pivotal role in ensuring these rules are properly observed.

The custody officer
The custody officer is responsible for safeguarding the rights of suspects at the police station. Section 36(5) stresses his independence allowing only minimal involvement at an earlier stage of the investigation.

His main duties are:
(a) to determine if the suspect's detention is valid. If not he should be released with or without bail (s.34(1));

(b) to determine whether there is sufficient evidence to charge him (s.37(1)). He must not delay charging to allow questioning to continue;

(c) if the suspect is not charged the custody officer may be required to release him. The presumption is that the suspect will be released with or without bail, but it can be rebutted if the custody officer has reasonable grounds for believing that detention without charge is necessary to secure or preserve evidence relating to the offence for which the suspect has been arrested, or to obtain such evidence by questioning him (these are often referred to as the "detention conditions" and are set out in s.37(2));

(d) to keep the custody record which records the history of the detention (s.39(1)(b) and para.2 of the Code). The record is available to a solicitor or appropriate adult on arrival at the station and to the suspect on request for 12 months;

(e) to ensure that the suspect is treated in accordance with the provisions of the Act and the Code of Practice (see below);

(f) to itemise the suspect's property (see above);

(g) to inform the suspect of the reason for the detention, of his right to legal advice and his right to have a person informed that he is in custody and his right to consult the Codes of Practice. He should not, however, put specific questions to the suspect regarding his involvement in any offence, etc.

The right to legal advice and to have a person informed

A person who is in police detention is entitled to consult a solicitor privately at any time (s.58). The suspect must be told of this right both orally and in writing and will be asked to sign the custody record saying that this has been done. The availability of legal aid must be drawn to his attention and a poster outlining the right to legal advice must be displayed prominently in the charging area. The Code of Practice stresses that no attempt should be made to dissuade a person from obtaining legal advice.

The suspect also has the right to have one person informed that he is in custody. That person may be a friend, a relative or other person who is likely to take an interest in his welfare (s.56, para.5 of the Code).

These are not absolute rights in that in the case of indictable offences the s.56 right can be postponed for up to 36 hours on the authority of an officer of at least the rank of inspector and in the case of s.58, a superintendent, if that officer has reasonable grounds for believing that the exercise of either right would:

(a) lead to interference with evidence connected with an indictable offence or interference with or physical injury to other persons;

(b) "tip off" suspects;

(c) hinder the recovery of property;

(d) hinder the recovery of proceeds from drug trafficking.

Delay may also be authorised under the **Terrorism Act 2000**.

It is not sufficient reason for postponement of these rights that a solicitor might advise his client to remain silent (*R. v Neil McIvor* (CC, 1987)). There must be a belief that the solicitor would commit the criminal offence of alerting other suspects or be hoodwinked into doing so inadvertently or unwittingly. In *R. v Samuel* (CA, 1988), the court felt that either belief could only rarely be genuinely held by the police and, if substantiated, the suspect should be offered access to another solicitor.

The exercise of these rights

The Code says that consultation with a solicitor can be in person, in writing or by telephone. Note the use of the Duty Solicitor Scheme and the provision of free legal advice. About one third of suspects exercise this right. For this purpose advice can be given either by a solicitor or by an accredited representative, i.e. one who is on a register of representatives maintained by the Legal Services Commission.

Even where there is an absolute right to legal advice, the suspect can be questioned before that advice is given if he consents, or where waiting would cause unreasonable delay or hindrance.

Solicitors are usually present during the suspect's interview but the Code says that they may be asked to leave if their conduct prevents the investigating officer properly questioning the suspect. Such an exclusion might entail the solicitor being reported to the Law Society as it is seen as a serious step.

Where a relative or friend of a person in custody inquires as to his whereabouts, that person should normally be told unless the detainee objects or unless any of the factors, noted above, justifying delay, apply. The Code provides additional safeguards for juveniles, mentally disordered and mentally vulnerable persons, the deaf and those who cannot speak or understand English (see for example, paras 3.12 and 3.13 of Code C.)

The interview

It is the responsibility of the custody officer to ensure that detainees are treated in accordance with the Act and the Codes of Practice (s.39(1)).

Under para.12.1 of the Code, the custody officer has the power to decide whether the suspect can be interviewed by another officer. In the case of a dispute between the custody officer and investigating officer (who may often outrank him), s.39(6) provides that the matter should be referred to an officer of the rank of superintendent or above. The Code requires that there be an adequate record of the interview, that the suspect is given refreshments and allowed periods of rest during extended questioning. Paragraph 12.2 provides that, in any 24-hour period, a suspect must normally be given eight hours' rest. This should normally be at night. Questioning must not be oppressive. The purpose of any interview is not necessarily to obtain an admission but to obtain from the suspect his explanation of the facts.

As soon as the investigating officer believes that a prosecution should be brought and there is sufficient evidence for it to succeed, questioning should cease.

If a person is charged with an offence the police cannot question the defendant any further. There have been recent suggestions that the police should be able to question defendants post-charge. Keep an eye out for developments in this area.

Review of detention
An important safeguard introduced by **PACE** is the periodic review of detention to see if such detention is justified in terms of the detention criteria in s.37(2) noted above. After initial consideration by the custody officer, the responsibility for the reviews rests with the review officer who, under s.40(1)(b), must be an officer of at least the rank of inspector and who has not been directly involved in the investigation. Where a person has been arrested and charged, the review officer is the custody officer. The first review takes place not later than six hours from the time the detention was authorised. The second review should not be later than nine hours after the first, i.e. 15 hours after the detention was authorised. Subsequent reviews should take place every nine hours thereafter. In *Roberts v Chief Constable of Cheshire* (HC, 1999), failure to carry out a timely review of detention rendered the previously lawful detention unlawful and entitled the suspect to claim damages. The obligation to review continues throughout the detention period.

Limits on period of detention without charge
The initial period of detention is 24 hours but the superintendent responsible for the station where the detainee is being held can extend this period for a further 12 hours. To issue a warrant of continued detention he must have reasonable grounds to believe:

(a) that the suspect's continued detention is necessary to secure or preserve evidence relating to the offence for which he is under arrest or to obtain such evidence by questioning him (i.e. the detention conditions apply);
(b) that it is an indictable offence; and
(c) the investigation is being carried out diligently and expeditiously.

Further detention beyond the 36 hour point can only be authorised under a warrant of further detention issued by magistrates under s.43 if:

(a) it is an indictable offence;

(b) the detention conditions apply;

(c) the investigation is being conducted diligently and expeditiously.

This authorises further detention for periods up to 36 hours. Further applications can be made for extensions up to a maximum of 96 hours from the commencement of the detention. At 96 hours, the suspect must be either charged or released.

The detention clock

In calculating the time limits for detention, the starting point is:

(a) where a person has been arrested outside the police station;

    (i) the time he arrives at the relevant station; or

    (ii) the time 24 hours after the time of his arrest, whichever is the earlier;

(b) where a person attends the police station voluntarily and is subsequently arrested there, the time of arrest.

There are special provisions where a person is arrested in another part of the country or abroad.

Applications to a magistrate should, if possible, be made during normal sittings and, in any event, not between 9pm and 10am. Section 43(5) gives a six-hour leeway at the 36-hour point in that an application for a warrant of further detention can be made up to 42 hours from the commencement of the detention clock, in a situation where the 36 hour period runs out at a time when it is not possible for a magistrate's court to sit. If, however, it was reasonable for the police to make the application in time, the magistrates must dismiss any application made after the 36-hour point. (See *R. v Slough JJ. Ex p. Stirling* (HC, 1987)).

The suspect or his solicitor is entitled to make representations to the reviewing officer as to why he should be released. A decision to continue the detention must be recorded in the suspect's custody record with reasons. Where an application for further detention is sought, the suspect must be taken before the magistrates and provided with a copy of the police information against him. He has a right to legal aid and legal representation.

Section 306 of the Criminal Justice Act 2003 extends the period for which those suspected of terrorist offences under s.41 of the **Terrorist Act 2000** can be detained to 14 days without charge.

Detention after charge

Section 38(1) allows this:

(1) if necessary to substantiate a name or address;

(2) if the custody officer has reasonable grounds for believing this is necessary:

    (a) for the suspect's own protection;

    (b) to prevent him from causing physical injury to any other person;

    (c) to prevent loss or damage to property;

    (d) to ensure his appearance in court;

    (e) to prevent interference with the administration of justice or with the investigation of offences;

    (f) juveniles can also be detained in custody if the custody officer believes this to be in the juvenile's own interests.

Otherwise under s.46(2) the accused should be brought before a magistrate as soon as is practicable and, in any event, not later than the first sitting after he has been charged. There are detailed provisions for the arranging of special sittings if no regular court is scheduled for the day the accused is charged or the following day.

POWERS OF ENTRY AND SEARCH

Police powers to enter premises come from the following sources:

- consent of the occupier;
- under statutory power;
- by virtue of a warrant.

Premises are defined in s.23 of **PACE** and include any place and, in particular, any vehicle, vessel, aircraft, tent, etc.

Article 8(2) of the ECHR only permits a public authority to interfere with an individual's right to respect for his home etc, in accordance with the law and where necessary in a democratic society for the prevention of disorder or crime. To comply with this, any power of search must be clearly delineated and must be used proportionately. In *Hepburn v Chief Constable Thames Valley Police* (CA, 2002) the court emphasised that the power to search premises only existed when the conditions prescribed by law existed.

Thus Code of Practice B, which applies to all searches, states that as the right to privacy and respect for personal property are key principles of the **Human Rights Act**, powers of entry, search and seizure should be clearly justified. Powers should be exercised courteously, with respect for persons and property. Reasonable force may be used only where necessary and must be proportionate to the circumstances.

Consent

It is estimated that the largest proportion of entries and searches takes place following the consent of the occupier. In the past it has been alleged that consent was often less than genuine, the person believing that he had no option but to allow the police the right to enter the premises and search. Code of Practice B recognises that consent must mean real consent. The occupier must be told that he can refuse to allow the search and that anything seized may be used in evidence. It provides that if consent is given, it must, if practicable, be in writing. The police must satisfy themselves that the person is in a position to give such consent.

Statutory powers of entry

(a) To execute a warrant of arrest (s.17(1)(a)). To arrest for an indictable offence (s.17(1)(b)). To arrest for various offences under the Public Order Act 1986, the Criminal Law Act 1977, the Road Traffic Act 1988 etc. (s.17(1)(c)).

(b) To recapture a person who is unlawfully at large (s.17(1)(cb)) or whom the officer is pursuing (s.17(1)(d)).

(c) To save life and limb or serious damage to property (s.17(1)(e)). In *Blench v DPP* (DC, 2004) the police were entitled to enter a house where a distressed woman alleged that a drunken man was attempting to abduct a child. Shouting could be heard. The police were entitled to enter as there had been a clear risk to others.

(d) Although all other common law powers are abolished, s.17(6) retains the common law power of entry to deal with or prevent a breach of the peace (*Thomas v Sawkins* (HC, 1935)).

(e) There still exist other statutes which authorise the police and/or other officials to enter premises without a warrant, e.g. Customs and Excise Management Act 1979 s.84(5) which allows entry to a place where there are reasonable grounds to suspect signals or messages being sent to smugglers and various statutes giving powers of entry to electricity and trading standards officers and firemen. The precise requirements, such as the need for written authority, vary from statute to statute.

(f) Special provisions permitting covert entry by police, customs etc, are contained in the Police Act 1997.

Section 17 entry

Under s.17 officers can enter premises for the following reasons:

- to arrest someone under a warrant of arrest;
- to arrest someone for an indictable offence;
- to arrest someone for various offences set out in s.17 (1)(c);
- to recapture someone who is unlawfully at large;
- to save life or limb or to prevent serious damage to property.

The officer must have reasonable grounds to believe that the person is on the premises.

Statutory powers of search

(a) Following the arrest of a suspect for an indictable offence, there is a power under s.18 to search the suspect's premises for evidence relating to the offence, or some connected or similar offence. If necessary, a police officer can search under this section before taking the suspect to the police station (s.18(5)). Apart from this, such a search must be authorised by an officer of the rank of inspector or above. The phrase "similar" is likely to lead to difficulty.

Section 18 search

The following conditions need to be satisfied for the police to be able to conduct a s.18 search:

- they can only take place after a suspect has been arrested;
- the offence must be indictable;
- the premises must be occupied or controlled by the suspect;
- the officer must have reasonable grounds to suspect there is evidence on the premises;
- the evidence must either relate to the offence the suspect is under arrest for or a connected or similar offence;
- the search can only be to the extent that is reasonably required to find what is being sought;
- an officer of at least the rank of Inspector must have given written authorisation for the search before it is carried out;
- a search can be carried out before the suspect is taken to the police station and without written authorisation only if the suspect's presence at the property at that time is necessary for the effective investigation of the offence. If this happens, written authorisation must be sought from an Inspector or above as soon as possible;

- whoever authorises the search must make a written record of the ground of the search and the evidence that is being sought;
- officers are authorised to seize any items they are allowed to search for under this section.

(b) Section 32(2)(b), dealing with the search of anyone arrested for any offence, indictable or otherwise, allows the police to enter and search the premises where the suspect was at the time of his arrest or immediately before for evidence relating to the offence for which he was arrested. The search must be no more than reasonably required for the purposes of discovering such evidence and there must be reasonable grounds for believing that such evidence will be found. This is an immediate power which must be exercised at the time of the arrest (*R. v Badham* (1987)).

Section 32 search

The following conditions need to be satisfied for a s.32 search to be carried out lawfully:

- an officer can search a person upon arrest (as long as they were arrested at a place other than a police station) if he has reasonable grounds to believe that the person is a danger to themselves or others;
- an officer may also search the person for anything that might assist the person to escape from custody or that might be evidence of an offence if he has reasonable grounds to believe that the person has such items in his possession;
- searches of the person under this section only allow searches outer clothing. Only outer coat, jacket or gloves can be removed. A search of a person's mouth is allowed under this section;
- if the offence the person has been arrested for is an indictable offence the officer may also enter and search any premises that the person was in when he was arrested, or that he was in immediately before he was arrested;
- the officer can only enter and search such premises for evidence relating to the offence the person has been arrested for;
- the search can only be to the extent that is reasonably required to find what is being sought;
- the officer can only carry out such a search of premises if he has reasonable grounds to believe that he will find such evidence on the premises;

- officers have seizure powers for anything that they are allowed to search for under this section or that they reasonably believe is evidence of an offence or has been obtained in consequence of an offence.

Search warrants

There are a number of Acts of Parliament which empower a magistrate on sworn information to issue a warrant to search for such things as stolen goods, forged documents or drugs. The most general power to obtain a warrant, a power which was extended by the Serious Organised Crime and Police Act 2005, is contained in s.8 of **PACE**. To issue such a warrant, the magistrate must be satisfied that an indictable offence has been committed, that there is material on the premises which is likely to be of substantial value to the investigation, that it is relevant and that one of the conditions specified in s.8(3) applies. These conditions include the inability to obtain permission to enter and search or the need to carry out an immediate search in order to prevent the potential evidence being lost or destroyed. The warrant should identify the legal authority for the application, the premises to be searched, the object of the search and the grounds for undertaking the search.

Items subject to legal privilege, excluded material and special procedure material are not available under a s.8 warrant.

Section 8 search warrant
- Police apply to Magistrates.
- Magistrates issue warrant if they are satisfied there are reasonable grounds to suspect:
  - an indictable offence has been committed;
  - there is material on the premises that are likely to be of substantial value to the investigation of the offence;
  - the material is likely to be relevant evidence;
  - the material is not subject to legal privilege, excluded material or special procedure material.

And:
- It is not practicable to communicate with anyone who can grant entry to the premises or the material concerned.
- Entry will not be granted to the premises unless a warrant is issued.
- The purpose of the search may be frustrated or seriously

prejudiced if a person who can grant access to the material knows beforehand that a search is going to be carried out.
- Officers can seize anything that they have been authorised to search for.

Items subject to legal privilege

This broadly relates to communications between lawyer and client either in relation to the giving of legal advice or in contemplation of legal proceedings. In *R. v Snaresbrook Crown Court Ex p. DPP* (DC, 1988), a legal aid application was held to be subject to legal privilege. Items held with the intention of furthering a criminal purpose are excluded from this category (see *R. v Central Criminal Court Ex p. Francis and Francis* (HC, 1988)). No warrant can be obtained to seize such material. Even if the police "chance" upon it in the course of a legal search, it cannot be taken.

Excluded material

As defined in s.11, this includes journalistic material held in confidence and confidential personal records held by such people as doctors, social workers, etc. No new rights to such material are given by the Act but it does standardise the procedure for applying for a warrant to obtain such material. Applications must be made to a circuit judge. In *R. v Central Criminal Court Ex p. Brown* (DC, 1992), it was held that a judge had no power to issue a warrant to obtain hospital records under s.9 as there had been no right to obtain the materials before **PACE**.

Special procedure material

This consists of other types of confidential material which does not fall within the definition of excluded material in s.11. It includes material held in confidence which is not classed as "personal records" and certain types of journalistic material not caught by the definition in s.13. Access to special procedure material can only be obtained by virtue of a warrant issued by a circuit judge. For examples see *R. v Bristol Crown Court Ex p. Bristol Press and Picture Agency Ltd* (HC, 1987) and *Re An Application under s.9 of the Police and Criminal Evidence Act 1984* (HC, 1988).

The conduct of the search

Code B emphasises:
- (a) searches must be made at a reasonable hour unless this might frustrate the purpose of the search (para.5.2);
- (b) unless impossible or it would, for example, frustrate the search by losing the element of surprise, the police should attempt to explain to

the occupant the authority for the search and obtain consent. In *O'Loughlin v Chief Constable of Essex* (CA, 1988), failure to do this meant that the police were trespassers;

(c) where such consent is refused or the premises are unoccupied, reasonable force may be used to effect entry. In *Murgatroyd v CC of West Yorkshire* (CA, 2000), the use of a police dog in forcing an entry under s.17(1)(e) was considered an unreasonable use of force;

(d) any occupier should be served, where practicable, with a standard notice of powers and rights. This explains the basis on which the search was made and explains the rights of the occupier;

(e) premises may not be ransacked but searched only to the extent necessary to achieve the objects of the search;

(f) searches must be conducted with due consideration;

(g) the search should be discontinued if it becomes clear that the items sought are not on the premises.

If it is thought that the search might have an adverse effect on good community relations, the officer in charge should normally consult the local police community relations officer before proceeding with the application.

The extent of the search and seizure

Where the police are searching by virtue of a warrant, s.16(8) states that the search may only be to the extent required for the purpose for which the warrant was issued. Where entry is justified under s.17, the power to search is only to the extent reasonably required for the purpose for which the power of entry was exercised.

Section 18 allows the police to search for evidence relating to the offence for which the suspect has been arrested or evidence relating to some other indictable offence which is connected with or similar to that offence. The s.32 power is narrower in that it only permits premises to be searched for evidence relating to the offence for which the suspect has been arrested.

In all instances there is an accompanying power of seizure. In addition where the police chance upon evidence for which they had no power to search, the common law gave further powers of seizure. In *Ghani v Jones* (CA, 1970) additional powers of seizure would be given if there were reasonable grounds for believing that a serious crime had been committed, so serious that it was of first importance that offenders be brought to justice, that the item seized was the fruit of crime or material evidence to prove the commission of the crime, that it was unreasonable for the person in possession of the evidence to refuse to hand it over and that it was not kept any longer than necessary by the police. **PACE** s.19 may also give a power of seizure. If the police are lawfully on the premises they may seize other evidence if they have reasonable grounds to believe either that it has been obtained in consequence of the commission of an offence or that it is evidence in relation to an offence which they are investigating or any other offence. In either case the officer must have reasonable grounds for believing that it is necessary to seize the evidence there and then to prevent it being destroyed.

In *Cowan v The Commissioner of Police for the Metropolis* (CA, 1999) it was held that s.19 covered seizure of a vehicle. A vehicle falls within the definition of "premises" and where the nature of the premises made it physically possible for these to be seized and where practical considerations made this desirable, such a seizure was permissible.

The Criminal Justice and Police Act 2001 allows the police to remove items for sifting and examination elsewhere when it is not practical to do this on the spot.

Effect of non-compliance with PACE
Evidence obtained in breach of **PACE** and the Codes may be excluded by virtue of ss.76 and 78. A distinction is drawn between confession and other evidence.

Section 76 confessions
If it is alleged that a confession has been obtained by oppression or in consequence of anything likely to render it unreliable, the court will not admit it unless the prosecution can prove beyond reasonable doubt that it was not obtained in this way. Oppression may include torture, degrading treatment or the use or threat of violence. It may also arise from "the exercise of authority in a burdensome, harsh or wrongful manner; unjust or cruel treatment" (see *R. v Fulling* (CA, 1987)).

Bullying or hectoring by police officers might also constitute oppression (*R. v Paris* (CA, 1982)).

In determining whether anything said or done was likely to render a confession unreliable, the character of the accused will be relevant. So, for example, failure to allow access to a solicitor may constitute oppression in the case of an accused of low intelligence but may not if he is an experienced offender. (See *R. v Alladice* (CA, 1988) and *R. v Weeks* (CA, 1994).)

Section 78
The court has a discretion to exclude any evidence, including confessions, if it appears to the court, having regard to all the circumstances, that its admission would have such an adverse effect on the fairness of the proceedings that the court ought not to admit it. Failure to comply with provisions of **PACE** and the accompanying Codes of Practice might be considered to have such an effect. This will be particularly likely if there has been a

series of breaches. In *R. v Canale* (CA, 1990) the court exercised its discretion to exclude evidence where the breaches were seen to be "flagrant, deliberate and cynical". In *R. v Keenan* (CA, 1990) the court said that, to persuade the court to exercise its discretion to exclude evidence, the breaches must be "significant and substantial". Such breaches as denial of access to a solicitor (*R. v Samuel* (COA, 1988)) and failure to tell a suspect of his right to legal advice (*R. v Absolam* (CA, 1989)) have been viewed as particularly serious. Evidence has also been excluded as a result of failing to keep a proper record of the interview (*R. v Walsh* (CA, 1989)) and a series of breaches of the Code which, whilst individually were minor, cumulatively were sufficient to cast doubt on the fairness of the proceedings (*Canale*, above).

The use of such evidence may also be subject to challenge as a breach of Art.6 of the ECHR in that its admission interferes with the right to a fair trial.

Summary of important PACE provisions	
PACE section number	**Power**
1	Stop and search
2	Formalities of stop and search
3	Records of stop and searches
8	Search warrants
17	Powers of entry
18	Search of a suspect's premises after arrest
19	General seizure power
24	Arrest without a warrant
24A	Citizens' arrest
28	Formalities of arrest
30	Suspect must be taken to designated station as soon as possible after arrest
32	Search of suspect and/or premises they were in at time of arrest
34	Limitations upon detention
36	Creation of Custody Officer
37	Duties of CO pre-charge
38	Duties of CO post-charge
39	Responsibilities of CO for detainees

40	Review of detention
41	Time limit of detention
54	Search of detainees
56	Right to have someone informed of the suspect's detention
58	Right to legal advice
76	Excluding confession evidence
78	Excluding any unfair evidence
117	Powers of officers to use reasonable force

Summary of the Codes of Practice

PACE Code	Covers
A	Stop and Search
B	Entry, search and seizure
C	Detention, questioning and treatment of suspects at the police station
D	Identification
E	Audio recording of interviews
F	Visual recording of suspects
G	Arrest
H	Terrorism powers

POLICE MISCONDUCT

Remedies for unlawful arrest and detention

A basic principle of the rule of law is that any interference with the liberty of the individual must be justified by law. Simply by virtue of his official position no police officer has the right to interfere with a person's liberty unless he can point to legal authority to justify his actions. If a person is detained irregularly or his property or person searched without lawful authority, he has the following remedies:

1. Self-defence. If a person is unlawfully restrained he is entitled to use reasonable force to effect his escape (*Kenlin v Gardner* (HC, 1967)). This remedy must be pursued with caution as the amount of force used must be no more than is reasonable in the circumstances. If excessive

it may constitute an assault (*Fagan v MPC* (HC, 1968)). This may not be a very nice judgment to make in a stressful situation.

2. An action of damages may be brought for false imprisonment, wrongful arrest, etc.
3. An application for a writ of habeas corpus. The system of review of detention introduced under **PACE** does not affect the system of applications for habeas corpus. An ex parte application is made, supported by an affidavit.
4. Action of damages for trespass to the person, or trespass to goods.
5. A person whose chattels have been seized by the police can apply for an order for delivery of the goods and damages under s.3 of the Torts (Interference with Goods) Act 1977.
6. Complaint against the police.

It should be noted that breach of the Codes of Practice does not, of itself, render the police officer liable to any criminal or civil proceedings. The court can, however, take such a breach into account where relevant.

Complaints against the police

It was felt by the Royal Commission on Police Powers that criminal prosecution and investigation could only work well if the general public felt confident in the role played by the police. Before 1976 investigation of complaints was essentially an internal police matter. In 1976 the Police Complaints Board was established with limited functions to oversee the disciplining of police officers who had contravened the Police Disciplinary Code but had not faced criminal charges. It had no powers in relation to criminal actions against the police and no powers of investigation. In 1984 it became known as the Police Complaints Authority with greater supervisory powers. Nevertheless public confidence in the system remained low particularly among members of minority ethnic communities. A number of well publicised cases have illustrated the difficulties facing investigations of complaints where there are no independent witnesses. A further concern related to the number of complaints withdrawn before investigation leading to fears that undue pressure was being brought to bear on complainants.

The reluctance of the DPP to prosecute police officers has also attracted criticism. He operates on the basis that there must be a reasonable prospect that a jury is more likely to convict than acquit on the evidence. The DPP has said that experience has shown that stronger evidence is required than is the norm.

A new system for dealing with complaints was established under the **Police Reform Act 2002** which set up the Independent Police Complaints Commission (IPCC). It has the power to conduct investigations itself or manage or supervise police investigations. It also has a wider responsibility to monitor and work to improve the way in which all complaints are handled by local police forces. The chair is appointed by the Crown and the members by the Home Secretary.

Complaints may be brought by anyone who feels he is the victim of misconduct, anyone witnessing misconduct or any friend or representative of the victim. The system covers all ranks but does not deal with complaints about general policing policy.

The method of dealing with the complaint will depend on its nature. The majority of complaints are relatively minor and relate to such things as incivility. These are handled locally through a system of informal resolution, subject to the consent of the complainant. Complaints that require a formal investigation will either be investigated by the police or, in more serious cases, by the IPCC itself (Sch.3). The IPCC can supervise police investigations in certain circumstances and there is a right of appeal to it if the complainant is dissatisfied with the findings or the proposed outcomes of the investigation.

The decision whether to initiate criminal proceedings is taken by the DPP to whom allegations of criminal conduct must be reported.

Revision Checklist

You should now know and understand:

- the law relating to PACE stop and searches;
- the law relating to powers of arrest;
- the safeguards surrounding suspects' detention and questioning at the police station;
- the different laws relating to powers of entry, search and seizure.

QUESTION AND ANSWER

The Question

One evening the police receive reports that two youths have stolen cigarettes and some money from an old age pensioner who had just bought them at a local corner shop. He described them as quite small, wearing dark shell suits and one had a red baseball cap. Half an hour later PC Smith sees three boys smoking outside the shop. They are known to him as "troublemakers". They are all wearing shell suits but none are wearing caps.

He orders them to turn out their pockets which they grudgingly do. Nothing untoward is found. While the search is taking place, one of the youths ostentatiously drops a crisp packet on the ground at the officer's feet. He refuses to pick it up and tells the officer what to do with the crisp packet! At this point the officer bundles the youth into a police car and tells him he is under arrest.

Consider the legality of the police conduct.

Answer Guide

1. Consider whether PC Smith has the power to order the youths to turn out their pockets.
   (i)   There may be a power to stop and search for stolen goods under s.1(2)(a) of **PACE 1984**.
   (ii) The officer must have reasonable grounds for suspecting that he will find stolen goods (s.1(3)).
   (iii) Code of Practice on Stop and Search emphasises that whether the police have reasonable grounds for the stop and search depends on the circumstances of the case but they must have an objective basis, i.e. one which would appear justifiable and reasonable to a third party. Thus PC Smith can rely on the description of the alleged offenders, their presence in the vicinity, their demeanour. He can take into account his knowledge of them in conjunction with the other information noted above. He cannot rely on personal factors alone e.g. their bad reputation plus appearing a stereotyped offender.

You should reach a conclusion on this noting that the fact nothing was found is irrelevant. It was whether the officer had reasonable grounds at the time he embarked on the search.

2. Assuming there was a power to stop and search, has the search been carried out properly in terms of the Act?
   (i)   The search should be carried out courteously.
   (ii) If PC Smith is not in uniform, he must supply documentary evidence (s.2(2)(b)).
   (iii) He should have provided the information required in s.2(3).
   (iv) Having carried out the search, PC Smith should have completed a record of the search in accordance with s.3 and recorded the

information required in s.3(6). There appears to be no reason to exclude this requirement under s.3(1) or to delay making it under s.3(2).

(v) The power would entitle the police officer to ask the boys to turn out their pockets. He has not infringed s.2(9)(a).

It appears that while the extent of the search was lawful, the formalities which are designed to protect suspects have not been complied with.

3. The validity of the "arrest" grounds?

The police may arrest without a warrant if the officer knows an offence has been committed and that the youths have committed it (s.24(3)) and he has reason to believe an arrest is necessary under s.24(4). It is not clear from the facts that any of the factors listed in s.24(5) would apply in this case.

4. In addition the formalities for a valid arrest do not appear to have been complied with.

(i) The youth has been informed that he is under arrest (s.28(1)).

(ii) He has not been informed of the grounds of the arrest (s.28(3)). This is required even if the facts are obvious (s.28(4)). There appears to be no justification for delaying the giving of this information in accordance with s.28(5).

(iii) Consider whether the officer has used unjustifiable force.

Protest and Public Order

6

INTRODUCTION

In this chapter we will look at the following:
- the "right" to demonstrate;
- the powers of the police under the Public Order Act 1986 to regulate demonstrations;
- the common law phenomenon of Breach of the Peace;
- public order offences under the Public Order Act 1986;
- responsibility for the Police forces in England and Wales.

These five areas interlink as they examine the relationship between the police and the citizen. The focus of the chapter is upon the powers that the police exercise over the citizen in relation to demonstrations. Citizens are able to demonstrate, and the police need powers to be able to limit this ability to demonstrate in certain circumstances, such as where a demonstration has turned violent. We will examine some of the powers that the police have in this area and look at where the legal line is between being left alone to demonstrate and when the police can lawfully interfere with this ability.

THE "RIGHT" TO DEMONSTRATE

The right to demonstrate against unpopular causes has long been considered a bulwark of liberty in any civilised society, enabling groups within that society to attempt to influence public opinion, to express their solidarity, to pressurise government and publicise their cause. Accordingly, the constitutions of many states contain guarantees of the right of peaceful protest.

In the United Kingdom there was no such positive statement of the right to demonstrate although prior permission was not traditionally required. For example, an assembly or procession was not unlawful per se, unless it caused an obstruction or constituted a public nuisance. There was no obligation on the police to facilitate peaceful protest. Their fundamental duty was to preserve public order and they had wide ranging powers at their disposal to achieve this. There were numerous offences which could be contravened in the course of a demonstration. The law, rather than facilitating the right of peaceful protest, simply accepted that demonstrators could do what they liked providing they did not break the law, something it was very easy to do.

One basic restriction stemmed from the fact that the public was entitled to use the highway only for passage from one place to another and for matters incidental to that. In *Harrison v Duke of Rutland* (HC, 1893), it was held that a person who used the highway other than for passage could be sued for trespass. What constituted an approved incidental use appeared to be construed very narrowly. Improper use of the highway might also constitute a nuisance leading to criminal charges, a civil action of damages or an injunction prohibiting the continuation of the improper use. For example, a demonstration outside a firm of estate agents was prohibited, although peaceful (*Hubbard v Pitt* (HC, 1976)). In practice most demonstrations went ahead providing they were peaceful, well-organised and there was no actual obstruction.

This is an area of law which has seen considerable change in recent years. Following the passage of the **HRA** there has been a much more liberal approach to peaceful demonstrations. However, this has been countered in recent years by new restrictions imposed in response to terrorist attacks.

The ECHR and the Human Rights Act

Article 11 of the ECHR says that everyone has the right of peaceful assembly and to freedom of association with others. Although not absolute rights, no restriction must be placed on the exercise of these rights except where prescribed by law and necessary in a democratic society in the interests of national security or public safety, for the prevention of disorder or crime, for the protection of health or morals or the protection of the rights and freedoms of others. Article 10 of the ECHR provides that everyone has the right to freedom of expression (again subject to the same qualifications). As public authorities, the police and the courts must act in a manner which facilitates the right of peaceful protest and any restrictions imposed must be for the purposes stated in the convention and must be proportionate.

The change of approach necessitated by these provisions was anticipated in *DPP v Jones* (HL, 1999). Jones had been convicted of trespassory assembly following a peaceful protest on the highway near Stonehenge. The House of Lords by a majority allowed the appeal, stating that a peaceful assembly on the highway did not necessarily exceed the public's right of access. Lord Irvine went further than the other judges in recognising a right of peaceful assembly on the highway saying that, otherwise, English law would be in direct conflict with the convention.

Art.10 ECHR
Freedom of Expression

1. Everyone has the right to freedom of expression. This right shall include freedom to hold opinions and to receive and impart information and ideas without interference by public authority and regardless of frontiers. This Article shall not prevent States from requiring the licensing of broadcasting, television or cinema enterprises.

2. The exercise of these freedoms, since it carries with it duties and responsibilities, may be subject to such formalities, conditions, restrictions or penalties as are prescribed by law and are necessary in a democratic society, in the interests of national security, territorial integrity or public safety, for the prevention of disorder or crime, for the protection of health or morals, for the protection of the reputation or rights of others, for preventing the disclosure of information received in confidence, or for maintaining the authority and impartiality of the judiciary.

Art.11 ECHR
Freedom of Assembly and Association

1. Everyone has the right to freedom of peaceful assembly and to freedom of association with others, including the right to form and to join trade unions for the protection of his interests.

2. No restrictions shall be placed on the exercise of these rights other than such as are prescribed by law and are necessary in a democratic society in the interests of national security or public safety, for the prevention of disorder or crime, for the protection of health or morals or for the protection of the rights and freedoms of others. This Article shall not prevent the imposition of lawful restrictions on the exercise of these rights by members of the armed forces, of the police or of the administration of the State.

THE POWERS OF THE POLICE TO REGULATE DEMONSTRATIONS

The **Public Order Act 1986** distinguishes between public processions and public assemblies. Public processions are defined in *Flockhart v Robinson* (HC, 1950) as a body of persons moving along a route. A public assembly is defined in s.16 as an assembly of two or more persons in a public place that is wholly or partly open to the air. By s.11 of the Act, anyone organising a march must give the police six days' notice otherwise he may commit an offence. When a march is organised at short notice, as much notice as is practicable must be given. The provision is designed to ensure that the policing of the demonstration can be properly planned. There is an exception for processions which are commonly or customarily held. In *Kay v Commissioner of Police of the Metropolis* (HL, 2008), the monthly "Critical Mass" cycle rides through London were held to be a customary procession and therefore were not required to give notice under s.11 of the **Public Order Act 1986** (the HL reversed the CA's decision from 2007 which held that they were not customary and did need to give notice).

DEFINITION CHECKPOINT
Procession
The **Public Order Act 1986**, s.16 defines a "procession" as a procession in a public place. This is not overly helpful. A more helpful definition can be found in the case of *Flockhart v Robinson* [1950] 2 KB 498 at 502, where Lord Goddard C.J. stated, "*a procession is not a mere body of persons: it is a body, of persons moving along a route.*"

DEFINITION CHECKPOINT
Assembly
The **Public Order Act 1986**, s.16 states a "Public assembly" means an assembly of two or more persons in a public place which is wholly or partly open to the air.

DEFINITION CHECKPOINT
Public Place
The **Public Order Act 1986**, s.16 defines a "public place" as any highway, and any place to which at the material time the public or any section of the public has access, on payment or otherwise, as of right or by virtue of express or implied permission.

Conditions

Section 12 of the Act gives the police the power to impose conditions on processions where there is a risk of serious public disorder, to prevent serious damage to property, serious disruption to the life of the community and to prevent intimidation. The nature of such conditions is not specified but may relate to route, size, timing, etc of the march as necessary. Organising or participating in a march in breach of any such conditions constitutes an offence.

Organiser of a Procession

A definition can be found in the case of *Flockhart v Robinson* [1950] 2 KB 498 at 502, where Lord Goddard C.J. stated:

> " 'Organized' is not a term of art. When a person organizes a procession, what does he do? A procession is not a mere body of persons: it is a body, of persons moving along a route. Therefore the person who organizes the route is the person who organizes the procession."

Under s.14 the police are given a similar power to impose conditions on public assemblies. However, a more limited range of conditions is specified. In the light of the **HRA** any such conditions must be proportionate (*R. (Brehony) v Chief Constable of Greater Manchester* (HC, 2005)). They must also be in accordance with the law otherwise they will fall foul of the **HRA**. (See *DPP v Brian Haw* (DC, 2007) where the conditions lacked clarity.)

The power to ban

If the s.12 powers are judged insufficient and there remains a risk of serious public disorder, there is a power, under s.13, to ban processions for any period up to three months. The Chief Officer of Police may apply to the local authority for a banning order which must be confirmed by the Home Secretary. It is an offence to organise, to participate in or to incite someone to participate in a banned march.

The ban is a blanket ban covering all marches or all marches of a particular class such as political marches. This has caused some concern as peaceful demonstrators may be prevented from marching because of the threat posed by a potentially disruptive counter-demonstration. Yet the suggestion that there should be a power to impose selective bans was rejected, neither police nor judges appearing willing to become involved in such a politically sensitive task, the exercise of which would certainly bring forth accusations of bias.

Summary of important Public Order Act 1986 provisions relating to demonstrations

Public Order Act 1986	Summary of provision
s.11	Notice requirements for processions
s.12	Power to impose conditions upon processions
s.13	Power to ban processions
s.14	Power to impose conditions upon assemblies

Other statutory powers

Section 70 of the **Criminal Justice and Public Order Act 1994** (the 1994 Act) introduced a power to ban trespassory assemblies for up to four days. These are defined as assemblies which involve at least 20 people, are held on land to which the public has limited or no rights of access and take place without the permission of the occupier of the land.

Application must be made to the local authority by the Chief Officer of Police on the basis that he believes that an assembly is intended to be held which might result in serious disruption to the life of the community or significant damage to land, building or monuments of historical, architectural or scientific importance. Such a ban may cover an area of not more than a five-mile radius.

Section 71 of the **1994 Act** gives the police a power to prevent persons proceeding to banned trespassory assemblies. Note also the s.60 power to stop and search in anticipation of violence detailed in Ch.4 above.

The Serious Organised Crime and Police Act 2006 imposes specific rules with regard to areas designated by the Home Secretary such as the area around the Palace of Westminster. Under s.133 notice must be given of any demonstration in such an area.

The courts may have to consider whether the exercise of these various statutory rights is incompatible with protestors' convention rights, which the courts, as public authorities, are under a positive duty to uphold.

BREACH OF THE PEACE

At common law, the police have the power to take whatever action is necessary during a demonstration to prevent a breach of the peace. There have been conflicting views over the years as to what constitutes a breach of the peace.

It has been defined as something more than a mere disturbance of the public calm or quiet. An element of violence was deemed essential in *R. v Howell* (CA, 1982), and in *Percy v DPP* (DC, 1994) where the court, in determining whether the appellant should have been bound over to keep the peace, said that the test was whether there was a real risk of violence or threatened violence occurring. (Contrast this with *R. v The Chief Constable of Devon & Cornwall Ex p. CEGB* (CA, 1981) where Denning M.R. said that there would be a breach of the peace whenever a person, lawfully carrying out his work, is unlawfully and physically prevented by another from doing it.)

The violence need not always stem from the demonstrators. In *Nicol and Selvanayagam v DPP* (HC, 1995), demonstrators attempting to disrupt an angling competition by throwing twigs into the water were arrested and subsequently bound over to keep the peace although no violence or threats of violence against the anglers took place. It was sufficient that their conduct was unreasonable and interfered with a lawful activity. A natural consequence of the conduct would be to provoke violence in others. On the other hand in *Redmond-Bate v DPP* (CA, 1999) the court held that the police had acted unlawfully in arresting a speaker on the steps of Wakefield Cathedral who was drawing a hostile crowd. It was felt that her conduct was not unreasonable. See also *Steel and Others v UK* (ECHR, 1999). These cases do little to clarify the situation where it is clear that peaceful conduct is going to result in violent conduct by others. When does it become unreasonable for the peaceful protester to refuse to stop their protest and co-operate with the police?

This power has been used by the police in a variety of ways; to ask demonstrators to leave the scene, even when acting peacefully (*Duncan v Jones* (HC, 1936)); to justify the removal of provocative emblems or banners (*Humphries v Connor* (IR, 1864)); to direct a procession en route if a breach of the peace is reasonably apprehended (Lord Scarman's Report on the Red Lion Square Disorders). One of the most controversial uses of the power is to prevent demonstrators reaching the scene of the demonstration, a use upheld by the courts in *Moss v McLachlan* (HC, 1984). The court held that, providing the police honestly and reasonably believed there was a real risk of a breach of the peace, they were entitled to take reasonable preventative action. What that action consisted of must depend on the imminence or immediacy of the threat to the peace. In *McConnell v Chief Constable of the Greater Manchester Police* (CA, 1990), the Court of Appeal confirmed that a breach of the peace could take place on private premises. If a meeting is held in private premises it should be noted that the police can insist on entering the premises even against the wishes of the organisers, if they have reasonable grounds to believe a breach of the peace is likely to occur (*Thomas v Sawkins* (HC, 1935)), a power confirmed in *McLeod v MPC* (CA, 1994).

Any such actions to prevent a breach of the peace must now be considered in the light of the **HRA**, the positive duty on the police to facilitate peaceful protest and the need to act proportionately. In *R. (Laporte) v The Chief Constable of Gloucestershire* (HL, 2006), the police detained a coach-load of demonstrators en route to an anti-war rally at an RAF base and forced the coach to drive back to London without stopping. It was held that while the police were unjustified in imposing these restrictions, such restrictions had to be justified as "necessary in a democratic society" for a number of limited objectives such as the protection of public order. An imminent breach to public order had not been identified here. There was no right to imprison the demonstrators on the bus. Contrast this with *Austin v The Commissioner of Police of the Metropolis* (HL, 2009) where demonstrators had been kept within a police cordon for several hours yet no breach of the demonstrators' convention rights occurred.

Other devices used in recent years to control public order situations have been dispersal orders under the Anti-Social Behaviour Act 2003 (*Singh v Chief Constable of West Midlands* (DC, 2005)) and the use of injunctions to prevent protesters invading Heathrow in 2007.

The way demonstrations are policed was put under the microscope after the G20 demonstrations which took place in London in 2009. Some people were injured and one person died during the demonstrations. This led to a review of the police tactics in dealing with demonstrations.

PUBLIC ORDER OFFENCES

The major public order offences were put on a statutory basis by the **Public Order Act 1986**:

Riot (section 1)
This is the most serious of the offences in the Act, and is triable only on indictment and attracts a maximum penalty of ten years' imprisonment.

> "Where 12 or more persons who are present together use or threaten unlawful violence for a common purpose and the conduct of them (taken together) is such as would cause a person of reasonable firmness present at the scene to fear for his personal safety, each of the persons using unlawful violence for the common purpose is guilty of riot."

In order to obtain a conviction, it must be shown that the accused intends to use violence or is aware that his conduct may be violent.

It should be noted that while 12 persons must be present who are using or threatening violence, only the person charged need be shown to have intended to use the violence. The offence can be committed by aiders and abettors as well as by principals (*R. v Jefferson* (CA, 1994)). It is unclear the extent to which the 12 need form a cohesive group. Section 8 says that violence means any violent conduct towards persons or property. It is unnecessary to produce a person who fears for his safety. The test is whether a hypothetical bystander of the requisite firmness would suffer such fear.

Violent disorder (section 2)
This is the normal charge for serious outbreaks of public disorder.

> "Where three or more persons who are present together, use or threaten unlawful violence and the conduct of them (taken together) is such as would cause a person of reasonable firmness present at the scene to fear for his personal safety, each of the persons using or threatening violence is guilty of violent disorder."

It should be noted that the persons present need not have a common purpose (*R. v Mahroof* (CA, 1988)) but that all three must be using or threatening violence (*R. v McGuigan & Cameron* (CA, 1991)); that once again it is unnecessary to produce a frightened bystander; and that unlike riot, it is sufficient to intend to threaten violence.

Affray (section 3)
This is intended to penalise fighting in that:

> "a person is guilty of affray if he uses or threatens violence towards another and his conduct is such as would cause a person of reasonable firmness present at the scene to fear for his personal safety."

Again no frightened bystander need be present. The standard is whether a hypothetical bystander of reasonable firmness would fear for his safety. (See *R. v Davison* (CA, 1992).) As with ss.1–2, the offence need not be committed in a public place. However, unlike the other offences under the Act, the violence must be directed against the person and must be more than mere threatening words. In *R. v Dixon* (DC, 1993), the accused ordered his Alsatian to "kill the officer". He appealed against conviction claiming that he had merely used words. The court, while accepting that the offence could not be committed by words alone, dismissed the appeal on the ground that the dog had been used as a weapon.

Threatening, abusive and insulting behaviour (section 4)

This replaced s.5 of the Public Order Act 1936 which had long been the main public order offence and which had been used in a wide range of situations including demonstrations, football hooliganism, "streaking" and industrial disputes.

> "A person is guilty of an offence if he:
> (a) uses towards another person threatening, abusive or insulting words or behaviour; or
> (b) distributes or displays to another person any writing, sign ... which is threatening, abusive or insulting ... with intent to cause another to believe that immediate violence will be used ... or to provoke (such) violence."

The consequences feared or provoked must be immediate, unlawful violence not violence at some unspecified future time. (*R. v Horseferry Road Stipendiary Magistrate Ex p. Siadatan* (DC, 1991).)

The phrase "threatening, abusive or insulting" is likely to be interpreted as under the **Public Order Act 1936**. In *Brutus v Cozens* (HL, 1973), Lord Reid said that the words must be given their ordinary English meaning. They must be more than vigorous or unmannerly. The audience must feel threatened, abused or insulted.

Under s.6(3) a person is guilty of an offence under s.4 only if he intends his words, behaviour or writing, etc. to be threatening, abusive or insulting or is aware that it may be threatening, abusive or insulting (*DPP v Clarke* (DC, 1991)). The offence can be committed in public or private, but the Act is drafted in such a way as to exclude domestic disputes (s.4(2)). (See *Atkin v DPP* (DC, 1989).) It should be noted that in this offence we are not dealing with the hypothetical bystander. The conduct must be directed to another person and it is the reactions of that other person which matter. The speaker must take his audience as he finds it (*Jordan v Burgoyne* (HC, 1963)).

Intentionally causing harassment, alarm or distress (section 4A)

Section 154 of the **1994** Act created a new offence which was designed primarily to deal with cases of serious racial harassment although not confined to use in this context. It makes it an offence to intentionally cause harassment, alarm or distress by using threatening, abusive or insulting words or behaviour. It is seen as more serious than the s.5 offence and attracts a maximum penalty of six months' imprisonment or a level 5 fine or both.

Offensive conduct (section 5)

This is used for minor acts of disorder such as shouting and swearing which are likely to cause alarm or distress, displaying abusive or insulting slogans or throwing over dustbins and banging on doors in the common parts of blocks of flats. It would cover those minor disturbances formerly dealt with under s.5 of the **Public Order Act 1936** but also types of anti-social behaviour which have not been criminalised in the past.

> "A person is guilty of an offence if he:
> (a) uses threatening, abusive or insulting words or behaviour, or disorderly behaviour; or
> (b) displays any writing sign or visible representation which is threatening, abusive or insulting, within the hearing or sight of a person likely to be caused harassment alarm or distress thereby."

In *DPP v Clarke, Lewis, O'Connell & O'Keefe* (DC, 1992) it was held that, for a conviction, the accused must intend their behaviour to be threatening, etc or be aware that it might be. It is not, however, necessary to prove actual harm or distress.

Section 5(4) gives the police the power of summary arrest for this offence if the person persists in the conduct after being warned to stop (see *Groom v DPP* (HC, 1991).)

The imprecision of this offence has caused concern in that it leaves the police considerable discretion as to what type of conduct is unacceptable and, indeed, a recent research study has shown wide variation in its use from one police force to another. In the context of a demonstration or industrial dispute, participants may well shout slogans which are abusive and are likely to cause distress to those who disagreed with the cause in question. The Law Commission proposing the offence had confined it to situations where the alarm or distress experienced was "substantial" but this requirement was dropped from the Act itself. The court in *DPP v Orum* (DC, 1989) accepted that in appropriate circumstances police officers could be caused the necessary "harassment, alarm or distress". The use of the section has been wide-ranging. In *Vignon v DPP* (DC, 1997) for example, it was used against a market stall holder who installed a camera to spy on customers in the changing room. In fact the greatest single use of the section relates to insults directed at the police.

Using s.5 to restrict protest may infringe rights under Art.10(2) of the

Convention. In *Percy v DPP* (2002), a conviction under s.5, which resulted from a demonstrator defacing a US flag during a demonstration against US foreign policy, was quashed as being in breach of Art.10. Contrast this, however, with *Harry John Hammond v DPP* (DC, 2004) where H, an evangelical Christian preaching in public and displaying signs condemning homosexuality and lesbianism, was convicted under s.5. His appeal on the ground that this was an unjustifiable restriction of his freedom of expression under Art.10 was rejected as the restriction was required in order to show tolerance to others.

The Crime and Disorder Act 1998 creates several more serious offences based on ss.4 and 5 where the conduct is racially aggravated.

Summary of important Public Order offences	
Public Order Act 1986	**Summary of provision**
S.1	Riot
S.2	Violent disorder
S.3	Affray
S.4	Fear or provocation of violence
S.4A	Intentional harassment, alarm or distress
S.5	Harassment, alarm or distress

Other public order offences

Sections 1 and 2 of the **Public Order Act 1936** make:

(1) the wearing of a uniform signifying association with a political organisation or with the promotion of any political objective an offence. For the rather wide definition of "uniform" see *O'Moran v DPP* (HC, 1975);

(2) the organisation or training of a body whose purpose is either:

    (a) to usurp the function of the police or the armed forces; or

    (b) to use or display force in an attempt to achieve a political objective, an offence.

The **Public Order Act 1986** does not codify the law and must be seen against a background of common law. There remain a number of other offences which can be used in a public order situation. These include obstructing the police in the execution of their duty (see s.89(2) Police Act 1996 and *Duncan v Jones* (1936)); obstructing the highway under s.137 of the Highways Act 1980; note also the use of binding over orders.

The location of meetings and demonstrations

Any meeting on private premises must have the consent of the owner. The ECtHR held in *Appleby v UK* (2003) that there had been no violation of Art.10 where the owners of a shopping mall refused to allow demonstrators to campaign on their premises against a proposed development. In the past the law has largely dealt with trespassers by way of civil action. The **Criminal Justice and Public Order Act 1994** indicated a clear movement towards criminal remedies. See for example the power to remove trespassers under s.61 which strengthens earlier powers and s.68 which is designed to deal with disruptive trespassers who interfere with lawful activities through disruptive, obstructive or intimidating behaviour by the creation of the offence of "aggravated trespass".

. . . .

RESPONSIBILITY FOR THE POLICE

There is no national police force in Britain. Instead there are 43 local forces historically based on the counties with various amalgamations. In London there is the Metropolitan Police. Although separate and independent, they share an increasing number of centralised resources such as the police national computer and the national reporting centre. There is a national pay structure and terms and conditions of employment. It is felt that the increased provision of services on a national basis will lead to increased centralisation. The **Police Act 1997** continued the trend with the establishment of a National Criminal Intelligence Service Authority, a National Crime Squad and a Police Information Technology Organisation. The Police and Justice Act 2006 establishes the National Police Improvement Agency.

Under the Police Act 1964 control of the police was shared between the Home Secretary, the Police Authority and the Chief Constable (Metropolitan Police Commissioner in London). This division of authority was referred to as a system of "tripartite control".

The Home Secretary had a general duty under the **1964 Act** to promote the efficiency of the police. In fact he had considerable power and influence which arose from his financial controls, his control over the appointment and dismissal of chief constables, control over training and equipment and his ability to regulate standards through the inspection system. In addition, extensive guidance was given by Home Office Circular.

Police authorities were local authority committees made up of two-thirds councillors and one-third magistrates. They had a statutory responsibility to maintain "an adequate and efficient police force for the area". This rather vague phrase had traditionally led them to concentrate on buildings and equipment although, during the 1980s, some police authorities tried to influence styles of policing, for example, by refusing to pay for certain types of riot control equipment. The decision in *R. v Secretary of State for the Home Department Ex p. Northumbria Police Authority* (HL, 1988), which confirmed the Home Secretary's power to provide such equipment if he so wished, severely limited this tactic as a method of control.

The Chief Constable had operational control and was subject to no-one for the way in which he deployed his resources.

The 1994 and subsequent reforms

The 1994 reforms, now consolidated in the **Police Act 1996** as amended by the **Police Reform Act 2002** and the **Police and Justice Act 2006**, were said by the Government to be driven by the need to give the Home Secretary more direct control over the strategy and framework for policing and to give police authorities more opportunity to take key decisions locally, setting their own budgets and determining local strategies for policing. Critics responded that the changes would increase centralised control of the police. It was alleged that the increased powers given to police authorities were illusory, that it was "responsibility without power".

The Policing and Crime Act 2009 attempted to address this by imposing a duty upon Police Authorities to take into account the views and opinions of the people in their area.

The role of the Home Secretary

Section 36 of the **1996 Act** imposes a duty on the Home Secretary to exercise his powers in a manner and to such an extent as appears to him to be calculated to promote the efficiency and effectiveness of the police. His specific powers include:

(a) the setting of national priorities and a national policing plan (s.1 of the **2002 Act**);

(b) the setting of performance targets for the achievement of these (s.38);

(c) the issuing of codes of practice for police authorities and for chief officers to promote efficiency and effectiveness;

(d) the power to give directions to police authorities to remedy failures by any police force to effectively discharge any of its functions and to direct the responsible police authority to take specified measures to remedy the breach (s.40);

(e) the power to give directions to police authorities following their failings (s.40A);

(f) the power to give police authorities directions as to the minimum budget they must set in any financial year;

(g) the power to require special reports (ss.43 and 44) and cause local inquiries to be held (s.49), and powers further strengthened by s.3 of the **2002 Act**;

(h) wide powers to make regulations re discipline, training, equipment, the government, administration and conditions of service (s.50);

(i) control over appointment and dismissal of Chief Constables and Deputies. (In 2004 the Home Secretary initiated procedures for the removal of the Chief Constable of Humberside following criticism of his force in the investigation which followed the Soham murders in the interest of efficiency and effectiveness and to maintain public confidence. This power was confirmed by the High Court.);

(j) financial controls exercised through the grant from central government (s.46); and

(k) inspection through Her Majesty's Inspectors of Constabulary.

The cumulative effect of these has been to increase the effective controls available to the Home Secretary.

Police authorities

For every police area there is a police authority. In most cases it is made up of nine councillors, three magistrates and five independent members. The independent members are appointed by the police authority from a list of suitable candidates. These are recruited by advert and then interviewed and selected by a panel representing the police authority, the Home Secretary and a third member chosen by the other two. This complicated procedure was introduced to alleviate fears that the Home Secretary would have too great an influence over police authorities.

The function of the police authority is outlined in s.6 of the Act which states that it shall be the duty of the police authority to secure the maintenance of an efficient and effective police force for the area. In doing this it has to have regard for strategic priorities set by the Home Secretary and its own local objectives, performance targets and local policing plan. This plan, the draft of which will have been produced by the Chief Constable following local consultation, will include a statement of policing priorities and the authority's financial allocations. An important function of the police authority is to monitor the force's performance against this plan and produce an Annual Report.

The Chief Constable

In the Metropolitan area of London, the Chief Officer of Police is the Metropolitan Police Commissioner. Otherwise, under s.10 each police force is under the direction and control of the Chief Constable and, as will be seen, the courts are extremely unwilling to interfere with the way he settles general policies and concentrates resources. It has been argued that the effect of the recent police Acts has been to restrict the freedom of the Chief Constable in that he has to produce a local policing plan which takes into account both national and local objectives and sets performance targets. Inevitably this must affect decisions on allocation of resources.

The courts

There are many illustrations of the courts' reluctance to interfere with the Chief Constable's operational decisions. In *R. v Metropolitan Police Commissioner Ex p. Blackburn* (CA, 1968), Lord Denning said that while chief officers of police are answerable to law, there are many fields in which they have a discretion with which the law will not interfere.

> "It is for the Chief Constable ... to decide in any particular case whether enquiries should be pursued or whether an arrest should be made ... It must be for him to decide on the disposition of his force and the concentration of his resources on any particular crime or area."

In *R. v Chief Constable of Devon and Cornwall Ex p. CEGB* (CA, 1981) the court refused to issue a mandamus ordering the Chief Constable to assist the CEGB in clearing a site of demonstrators who were impeding survey work for a new nuclear power station as it could not tell the Chief Constable how he should respond to the situation as it could not judge the explosiveness of the situation at the time. In *R. v Chief Constable of Sussex Ex p. International Traders Ferry Ltd* (CA, 1997), the court said that it would only interfere if the decision was irrational, so manifestly unreasonable that the court could interfere on "Wednesbury" grounds (see Ch.8)

The courts have also refused to interfere with a policy direction not to enforce a particular law. In *R. v Metropolitan Police Commissioner Ex p. Blackburn No.3* (CA, 1973) it was alleged that the Metropolitan Police Commissioner had issued an illegal policy directive in ordering his men not to enforce the provisions of the Obscene Publications Act 1959. The court refused to issue an order of mandamus on the ground that it had not been established that such a blanket directive had been issued and that it was within his rights to deploy his forces as he wished.

Quite clearly, however, he does not have unlimited discretion. He has a duty to enforce the law of the land. So, for example, the courts have indicated that they would interfere if a Chief Constable decided not to take action against housebreakers in any circumstances. (See also *R. v Oxford Ex p. Levey* (HC, 1987).)

Recent reform proposals

The coalition Government of 2010 produced a Home Office Consultation Paper titled "Policing in the 21st Century". This paper outlined a major shake-up of how policing is delivered in England and Wales. The system outlined above is to be completely overhauled. Possibly the biggest change is to the structure of local policing. The 43 different police forces will remain in place, but the Police Authorities themselves are going to be abolished. They will be replaced by elected Police and Crime Commissioners who will have the power to appoint, and have authority over, Chief Constables for their area.

This is a major change. The intention is to de-centralise power and hand it back to the local areas. The Commissioners will be directly elected by the local areas in May 2012 and they will hold their office for four years at a time. Commissioners will be responsible for the direction of the policing in their area and set targets for the Chief Constable of their area.

The Police Authorities used to oversee the budget and other adminis-trative duties of local forces. As the Police Authorities are being abolished, these tasks will be taken over by Police and Crime Panels who will oversee the work of the Commissioner. At the time of writing it appears the Panel members will be made up of local councillors and some independent members.

Revision Checklist

You should now know and understand:

- the legal position of citizens being able to demonstrate in England and Wales;

- the different laws and powers available to the police to regulate demonstrations;

- breach of the Peace;

- the range of public order offences under the Public Order Act 1986;

- how the police are governed.

QUESTION AND ANSWER

The Question

After a local derby football match, a pub called "The Grapes" filled up with supporters from both football clubs.

The supporters of the winning team started jeering the other fans which resulted in fighting taking place. At one end of the pub there were eight people fighting and at the other end of the pub, around the corner, six people were fighting.

The landlord called the police and all those involved in the fights were arrested. One man, Guy, who was not involved in any of the fights, was also arrested by the police. He swore at the officers telling them they were "useless fascist pigs". He was taken to the police station with the others.

Discuss the public order issues arising out of the above scenario.

Advice and the Answer

This question requires a discussion of various public order offences. As it is a problem question, the relevant law needs to be discussed and then applied to the facts of the scenario in order for conclusions to be made. Problem questions are assessing the ability to apply law to facts.

The following **Public Order Act 1986** offences need to be discussed:

- S1—Riot
- S2—Violent disorder
- S3—Affray
- S4—Fear or provocation of violence
- S5—Harassment, alarm or distress

A discussion of the common law phenomenon of Breach of the Peace also needs to be included. The main issues that need to be discussed in relation to these laws is set out below.

1. Riot

Twelve people are needed for this offence to be made out. Eight people are fighting in one end of the pub and six people at the other end. This means that more than twelve people are involved. The issue that needs exploring is the requirement that the twelve people have a "common purpose" for their use or threat of unlawful violence. A discussion of "common purpose" is needed. Case law, such as *R. v Jefferson* (COA, 1994) needs to be examined.

2. Violent disorder

Three people are required for this offence and there is no need for a "common purpose" to be established. A discussion of the elements of the offence are needed and then applied to the facts to come to a conclusion as to whether the supporters are guilty of this offence. This offence is easier to establish than riot and much more common.

3. Affray
Affray is the usual offence for fighting. A discussion of the elements of the offence is needed. As this scenario involves a lot of people though s.2 is more likely to be able to be established.

4. Fear or provocation of violence
The elements of this offence need to be discussed to see if Guy is guilty of committing it. The issue here is whether Guy's utterance would cause a fear of immediate unlawful force to be used against the police. From the words Guy used this appears unlikely.

5. Harassment, alarm or distress
Guy may be guilty of committing this offence so the elements of it need to be discussed. Guy is much more likely to be guilty of this offence than of a s.4 offence as there is no requirement for the apprehension of immediate unlawful force. The issue that needs to be examined is whether the utterance is "threatening, abusive or insulting" and whether the police officers or anyone else present was likely to have been caused harassment, suffered alarm or distress by what Guy said. An important point to remember though is that police officers have been held to be more firm than the person of reasonable firmness due to their training (*DPP v Orum* [1989] 1 WLR 88), so what may constitute an offence against a normal citizen may not be sufficient to constitute an offence against an officer.

6. Breach of the Peace
The fighting in the pub could also constitute a breach of the peace. Breach of the peace needs to be defined using case law (such as *R. v Howell*) and then explored to see whether the fighting does constitute a breach of the peace.

Judicial Review

7

INTRODUCTION

The ability of the courts to review the exercise of public functions is important in ensuring executive accountability and in the protection of the public. This chapter examines:
- just what judicial review is;
- who can apply for judicial review;
- what decisions are amenable to judicial review;
- the available remedies and their scope;
- the judicial review process.

WHAT IS JUDICIAL REVIEW?

Judicial review is a process which invokes the inherent supervisory jurisdiction of the High Court and allows the court to review the legality of decisions made by bodies exercising public law functions. These include:
- government ministers and departments;
- local authorities;
- inferior courts;
- tribunals;
- other administrative bodies.

It must be stressed that the courts are not challenging the merits of the decision but rather whether it is a decision the body is entitled to make. As Lord Brightman noted in *Chief Constable of North Wales Police v Evans* (HL, 1982):

> "Judicial review is concerned, not with the decision, but with the decision making process. Unless that restriction of the power of the court is observed, the court will in my view under the guise of preventing abuse of power, be itself guilty of usurping power".

Basis of Judicial Review

Historically, the basis of the court's intervention was the ultra vires doctrine. If a body exercising statutory powers went beyond the four corners of the Act, that is, beyond the powers conferred upon them by Parliament, then the court could intervene. In *Anisminic v Foreign Compensation Commission* (CA, 1968) Lord Diplock described such misuse of power as excess of jurisdiction.

The doctrine of ultra vires was used not simply to control the scope of the power being exercised but also to control the way it was used. So where a body used its power in a manifestly unreasonable manner, acted in bad faith, refused to take relevant factors into account in reaching its decision or based its decision on irrelevant ones, the court would intervene on the ground that the body had abused its power. (See Lord Reid in *Anisminic* (HL, 1969).) The basis of the control was that the courts considered that when Parliament gave a body statutory power to act, it could be implied that Parliament intended it to act in a particular way; in good faith, in a reasonable manner, in accordance with the requirements of natural justice. However, in attempting to control such abuse of power, the courts have blurred the distinction between the merits of the decision and its vires. This could be seen particularly in cases such as *Congrieve v The Home Office* (CA, 1976).

In recent years the courts have extended their supervisory jurisdiction beyond a review of the exercise of statutory powers to include the exercise of prerogative powers. The language of ultra vires is therefore no longer appropriate.

WHO IS AMENABLE TO JUDICIAL REVIEW?

The supervisory jurisdiction of the High Court is over bodies exercising public law functions and may include both bodies established by statute or through an exercise of the royal prerogative and private bodies. In *R. v City Panel on Take-overs and Mergers Ex p. Datafin Plc* (CA, 1987), it was held that decisions of an unincorporated association which exercised no statutory or prerogative powers were amenable to judicial review. Despite the fact that it was "a body performing its functions without any means of judicial support" (per Lord Donaldson M.R.), the nature of the power being exercised brought it within the supervisory jurisdiction of the High Court. The courts are therefore willing to look beyond the source of a body's powers (that is, whether they derive from statute or an exercise of the royal prerogative) and examine the nature of the powers being exercised to determine if it is amenable to judicial review. Lord Justice Loyd held that "if a body is exercising pubic law functions, or if the exercise of is functions have public law consequences, then that may be sufficient to bring the body within the reach of judicial review."

The justification for this is often that the body is carrying out a function, which, if it did not perform it, would be carried out by the Government. A further justification might be that the function is closely enmeshed with a public function (*Poplar Housing and Regeneration Community Association Ltd v Donoghue* (CA, 2002)). However, decisions being exercised by private bodies which have no public law functions will not be subject to judicial review. So, in *R. v Chief Rabbi Ex p. Wachmann* (DC, 1992), the court held that the exercise of a disciplinary function by the Chief Rabbi was not susceptible to judicial review.

Conversely, not every public body will be subject to review with regard to every action it takes, only if it is a public matter. (See *R. v BBC Ex p. Lavelle* (CA, 1983) which stressed that where public bodies carried out purely managerial functions, the exercise of such functions were not amenable to judicial review.)

WHO CAN APPLY FOR JUDICIAL REVIEW?

The requirements of standing to make a judicial review claim

Only a claimant who has the requisite standing may apply to the courts for judicial review. Section 31(3) of the Supreme Court Act 1981 provides that the court will not grant leave for judicial review unless the claimant has sufficient interest in the matter to which the application relates. However, the statute does not provide a definition of what amounts to a "sufficient interest" and the courts have therefore been called upon to determine the issue.

What constitutes sufficient interest?

KEY CASE

R. v IRC Ex p. The National Federation of Self Employed and Small Businesses Ltd (HL, 1982)

The applicants wished to challenge an alleged amnesty granted to casual workers in the newspaper industry who had been avoiding paying tax for many years. Quite clearly this decision did not affect the applicants' legal rights. But did they have a sufficient interest? Standing would be considered in two stages. Firstly at the filter stage, when leave to apply for review is sought and again when the court understood the legal and factual context of the case. The majority of the

House of Lords felt that the applicants' standing could not be considered in the abstract but only in conjunction with the merits of the case. Only in a few extreme cases could applications be weeded out for lack of standing at the filter stage. This case highlights the connection between the sufficiency of the interest and the seriousness of the illegality complained of. The more serious the illegality, the more liberal appear the rules of standing.

The House of Lords accepted that it was not necessary that the applicants' legal rights were affected, however, the court advised (Lord Diplock dissenting) that the IRC did not have sufficient interest in this case. According to Lord Scarman, the test was whether "there is a genuine grievance reasonably asserted", stressing the relationship between the sufficiency of the applicants' interest in relation to the subject matter of the application. Lord Fraser emphasised that a mere busybody would lack sufficient interest but gave little guidance as to how one distinguishes the busybody from the person with a reasonable concern.

Decisions since the IRC case have confirmed that a liberal approach to standing should be taken. Only claims by busybodies should be excluded.

- The interest of a business competitor was recognised in *R. v Department of Transport Ex p. Presvac Engineering Ltd* (CA, 1991).
- Persons have been deemed to have the requisite interest as a result of "legitimate expectation that they will be heard", perhaps arising out of assurances given or knowledge of general practice (*O'Reilly v Mackman* (HL, 1983)).
- Pressure groups have in many cases been allowed to apply for judicial review (*R. v Hammersmith & Fulham LBC Ex p. People Before Profit Ltd* (DC, 1981)). In *R. v HM Inspectorate of Pollution Ex p. Greenpeace* (DC, 1994) it was held that Greenpeace had standing to challenge the variation of existing authorisations for the Sellafield nuclear processing site by reason of its membership in the area.
- Claimants with "a sincere concern" for constitutional issues have also been deemed to have sufficient interest (e.g. where William Rees-Mogg was permitted to challenge the ratification of the Maastricht Treaty).
- Claimants raising issues of pubic importance have also benefited from liberal rules on standing. In *R. v Secretary of State for Foreign Affairs Ex p. World Development Movement* (HL, 1995), the question of standing was raised at first instance. Rose L.J. accepted that the applicants had standing on the basis of the importance of the issues raised, the likely absence of any other responsible challenger and the role of the applicant in giving advice on the grant of aid.

Thus in determining whether the applicant has standing, the courts consider:

- the merits of the application;
- the nature of the applicant's interest;
- all the circumstances of the case.

It must also be noted that s.7 of the **HRA Act 1998** requires that a claimant must be a "victim" of an unlawful act of a public body; a narrower test of standing.

The current procedural rules do not say anything new about standing but they give the court power to permit any person to file evidence or make representations at a hearing (CPR Pt 54(17)). This follows the approach which allowed Amnesty to make representations during the Pinochet hearing (*R. v Bow Street Magistrates Ex p. Pinochet* (HL, 1999)).

TIME LIMITS FOR MAKING AN APPLICATION

Under Pt 54(5) of the Civil Procedure Rules, a claim must be made promptly and in any event not later than three months after the grounds for the application first arose. This must be read together with s.31(6) of the **Supreme Court Act 1981** which says that the court may refuse an application for review on ground of undue delay if it considers that the granting of the relief would be likely to cause substantial hardship to, or substantially prejudice the rights of, any person, or would be detrimental to good administration. It would therefore appear that an application made within the three-month period could be refused for delay if, under s.31(6), the granting of the relief was, for example, detrimental to good administration (*R. v Dairy Produce Quota Tribunal Ex p. Caswell* (CA, 1989)), or if it would substantially prejudice the rights of another (*R. v Secretary of State for Health Ex p. Furneaux* (CA, 1994)).

The previous procedural rules under ord.53 did allow an extension to the three month period for good reason. For example, in *R. v Stratford-on-Avon DC Ex p. Jackson* (CA, 1985) the delay in making the application arose mainly because of difficulty in obtaining legal aid. The court was satisfied that the circumstances constituted a good reason for extending the period. In *Re S* (CA, 1997) where S had been detained under the Mental Health Act 1983, following her refusal to consent to a Caesarean section, the question was considered to be of such public importance that leave was granted despite the delay in applying. Rule 54(5) does not repeat this power to extend the period but there is a general power under r.3(1)(2)(a). Even if an applicant convinced the court that there was good reason for extending the three-month period, the application may still fail by virtue of s.31(6).

The short period available within which a claim may be brought, may render the time limits vulnerable to challenge under the **Human Rights Act** (*R. (Burkett) v Hammersmith & Fulham LBC* (2002)).

CLAIMS FOR REVIEW

The procedure for making claims for judicial review was introduced in October 2000 and can be found in Pt 54 of the Civil Procedure Rules (CPR). Judicial review procedure (JRP) is also subject to the overriding objectives contained in Pt 1 of the CPR.

The procedure for applying for judicial review

Judicial review is not automatically available, the permission of the court is necessary before the claim will be dealt with by the court ensuring that the valuable time of the court and the resources of bodies exercising public law functions are not wasted on vexatious claims.

There is therefore a two stage procedure for making the application (the judicial review pre-action protocol first requires the exchange of pre-action letters):

- application for permission;
- the hearing.

Application for permission

The purpose of this filter stage is to weed out hopeless cases at the earliest possible time, thus saving pressure on the courts and needless expense for the claimant. For example, it allows malicious and futile claims to be weeded out and prevents public bodies being paralysed for months because of pending court action.

In order to obtain leave, the claimant must satisfy the court that he has, on the face of it:
- an arguable case;
- the necessary standing to make the claim;
- brought the claim within the necessary time limits;
- no other remedy available.

The court will generally in the first instance consider a question of permission without a hearing. A hearing is likely to be requested if the claim involves a point of law likely to require some argument, if interim relief is sought or if the judge wishes to give guidance on a matter of public interest.

The notice of claim will be accompanied by an affidavit containing all the basic factual material on the application. The claim form must be served on the defendant.

Where permission is refused there is provision for renewal of the claim and a right of appeal. The exact procedure varies depending on whether it is a civil or criminal matter and whether there has been an oral hearing.

The requirement to seek permission is a significant filter but is being operated with considerable variation. Some judges examine the claim at length at this stage. Others content themselves with a quick look. Research has indicated that no common criteria are being applied. Despite this the new procedural rules say nothing about the criteria for the grant of permission.

The hearing

The hearing takes place in the Administrative Court of the Queen's Bench Division of the High Court and will normally be before two judges in a criminal case. In civil matters the case will normally be heard by a single judge sitting in open court. In very important cases, three judges may sit. It may even be decided without a hearing if the parties agree.

The main source of evidence will be sworn affidavits. The court has the power to take oral evidence and to permit cross-examination although this is unusual.

Claimants make an umbrella claim for judicial review. Within this claim, it is possible to ask for any of the remedies discussed below either singly, in any combination and in the alternative. See, for example, *R. v The Inland Revenue Commissioners Ex p. Rossminster* (HL, 1980). Damages can also be awarded where appropriate, e.g. for human rights breaches. Claimants do not have to choose which route to pursue, and may leave it to the court to provide the most appropriate remedy.

Discretionary nature of remedies

The court has a discretion as to whether to grant relief. Factors which might persuade the court to refuse the application are:

- the availability of an alternative remedy (*R. v Birmingham City Council Ex p. Ferrero Ltd* (CA, 1993), *Hossack v Legal Services Commission* (HC, 2010)). But if the alternative remedy is inappropriate in the circumstances the JRP may be used (*R. v Chief Constable of Merseyside Ex p. Calveley* (CA, 1986));
- where review would serve no useful purpose as the decision, properly taken, would be the same (*R. (on the application of H) v Essex CC* (CA, 2009), *R. v Monopolies and Mergers Commission Ex p. Argyll Group Plc* (CA, 1986));

- where the court does not like the motives of the applicant (*R. v Customs and Excise Commissioners Ex p. Cooke & Stevenson* (HL, 1970)).

Non-justiciability

Sometimes the courts will consider it inappropriate to exercise their power of judicial review on the basis that the nature of the dispute is such that it does not lend itself to resolution by a judicial type of process. This arises if the matter involves a balancing exercise which judges feel ill-qualified to perform. Examples given include disputes involving:

- the making of treaties;
- the defence of the realm; and
- the grant of honours (see Lord Diplock in the *CCSU* case).

However in *R. v Minister of Defence Ex p. Smith* (CA, 1996), it was said that:

> "only the rarest cases would today be ruled strictly beyond the court's purview, that is only those cases involving national security where the courts lacked the experience or material to form a judgement on the issues."

It has been suggested that the influence of the **Human Rights Act 1998** might be such as to prevent the court from refusing to interfere on this ground but in *Secretary of State for the Home Department Ex p. Isiko* (CA, 2001) it was emphasised that the concept of non-justiciability remained relevant and that there were still areas of judgements considered by democratically elected bodies which necessarily commanded deference from the courts. So, for example, in *R. (on the application of CND) v The Prime Minister* (2003), the courts refused to review the Prime Minister's decision to invade Iraq.

JUDICIAL REVIEW: THE AVAILABLE REMEDIES

The remedies available for those who seek a judicial review fall into two groups:

Perogative Orders	Non-Perogative Orders
☐ Quashing Orders	☐ Declarations
☐ Prohibiting Orders	☐ Injunctions
☐ Mandatory Orders	

The prerogative orders

These orders (formerly writs) were originally brought by the King against his officers to compel them to exercise their functions properly or to prevent them abusing their powers. They are remedies of public law. As such, historically, they were not available to control the activities of private bodies or domestic tribunals.

Quashing order

A quashing order (formerly certiorari), is used to quash the decisions of inferior courts, tribunals, government ministers, local authorities and other public bodies. In *R. v Northumberland Compensation Appeal Tribunal Ex p. Shaw* (CA, 1952) the tribunal, assessing the amount of compensation owed to Shaw, misinterpreted the statutory provisions and made an error of law which was apparent on the face of the record of the decision. That decision was quashed.

While formerly confined to judicial decisions affecting a person's legal rights, it has been granted to control licensing decisions (*R. v Barnsley MBC Ex p. Hook* (CA, 1976)); in *R. v Paddington Valuation Officer Ex p. Peachey Property Corp Ltd* (CA, 1966), to challenge an exercise of power by a valuation officer in compiling the valuation list; and in *R. v Hillingdon LBC Ex p. Royco Homes Ltd* (HC, 1974), to quash the granting of planning permission. It is clear therefore that quashing orders may now be sought to control the exercise of an administrative function, in addition to inferior courts and tribunals.

Prohibiting order

A prohibiting order (formerly prohibition) is used to restrain a tribunal, minister or other public body from proceeding in excess of jurisdiction. For example in *R. v Liverpool Corp Ex p. Liverpool Taxi Fleet Operators Association* (CA, 1972), it was alleged that a local authority had failed to exercise its discretion properly and was about to act illegally in the allocation of taxi cab licences. A prohibiting order was granted to prevent the authority acting on this invalid decision. In general its scope is similar to that of a quashing order.

Mandatory order

A mandatory order (formerly mandamus) is an order which commands a person or body to perform a public duty. Typically it is used to compel the exercise of a duty imposed by statute on a public body. For example, in *R. v Manchester Corp* (HC, 1911), the order compelled the local authority to make byelaws that it was under a statutory duty to make.

A mandatory order cannot be directed to the Crown as such as the

Crown is not commandable (*R. v Secretary of State for War* (CA, 1891)). However, where by statute, an officer of the Crown has an independent public duty towards a member of the public, the order may lie to compel performance of that duty. Thus a distinction is drawn between a duty imposed on the Crown and a duty imposed on a named Crown servant.

Non-prerogative orders

There are two remedies, the declaration and the injunction, which are not primarily remedies of public law but are widely used in this field.

Declaration

A declaration is a convenient and flexible remedy available in both public and private law matters which can be used to obtain a statement of the legal relationship between parties in a wide range of circumstances, without providing a remedy. It can be used, for example:

- to challenge the legality of administrative decisions (*Ridge v Baldwin* (HL, 1964));
- to challenge the validity of delegated legislation (*Daymond v South West Water Authority* (HL, 1976));
- to establish the existence or the scope of a public duty (*Central Electricity Board v Jennaway* (HC, 1959));
- to make declaratory judgments against the Crown.

It is not necessary for the claimant to show that he has some subsisting cause of action or a right to some other relief (*Gouriet v Union of Post Office Workers* (HL, 1978)). *R. v Secretary of State for Employment Ex p. Equal Opportunities Commission* (HL, 1994) made it clear that the court still has the power to make a declaratory judgment in judicial review proceedings whether or not it could also make a prerogative order.

Restrictions on the use of the declaration

- The claimant must have a right or interest which is justiciable.
- There must be a real dispute between the parties. The court will not attempt to resolve an academic matter (*R. v Secretary of State for Employment Ex p. Equal Opportunities Commission* (HL, 1994)).
- As a declaration will not quash a decision, it cannot be used to challenge a decision on the ground that there has been an error of law on the face of the record of the tribunal's decision as this is an error within jurisdiction. A declaration that such a decision is irregular would still leave the decision intact (*Punton v Minister of Pensions and National Insurance No.2* (HL, 1963)).
- Interim declarations cannot be made.

Injunction

This is an order by the courts, either prohibiting the party to whom it is addressed from doing a particular act, or requiring the party in question to perform a particular act. Accordingly injunctions can be either prohibitory or mandatory. It can be used:

- to prohibit a body from acting ultra vires. In *Bradbury v Enfield LBC* (CA, 1967) an injunction was granted to prevent a local authority from reorganising local schools without following the correct procedure;
- in *Att-Gen, ex relator McWhirter v IBA* (CA, 1973), an application was made for an injunction to restrain breaches of statutory duty;
- while mandatory injunctions are much less common in public law as mandatory orders are normally a more appropriate remedy, they have been granted, for example, to require public bodies to enforce planning regulations and fire precautions.

Restrictions on the use of the injunction

Under the Crown Proceedings Act 1947 s.21(1), a final injunction will not be awarded against the Crown or one of its officers, although this has little practical importance as the Crown will abide by the terms of a declaration. (The major difficulty has been the inability to obtain interim relief.) In the express context of Community law, the House of Lords in *Factortame Ltd (No.2)* (HL, 1991) disregarded the rule precluding such interim relief in national law, in order to give protection to the rights claimed under Community law. In *M v Home Office* (HL, 1994), the possibility of interim relief against ministers and government departments acting in the name of the Crown was recognised.

. . . .

AN EXCLUSIVE PROCEDURE?

Clearly the procedure described above must be used to obtain a prerogative order. But in the case of a declaration or an injunction, does the applicant have the choice in a public law matter to use another form of procedure?

In *O'Reilly v Mackman* (HL, 1982) an attempt to obtain a declaration by way of action that a Board of Visitors had acted contrary to the rules of natural justice in hearing disciplinary charges against a prisoner, was struck out as an abuse of process. Section 31(2) of the **Supreme Court Act 1981** provides that a declaration may be obtained by means of an application for review where the High Court considers it would be just and convenient having regard to:

- the nature of the matters in respect of which relief may be granted by way of the prerogative orders;

- the nature of the persons and bodies against whom relief may be granted;
- all the circumstances of the case.

The court was satisfied that, in the circumstances, relief could have been granted by way of a prerogative order. It was clearly a public law matter and would be more appropriate to use the JRP as it provided safeguards against frivolous applications, for example through the need to apply for leave. Their Lordships felt that although it was not the exclusive procedure for raising such a matter it would generally be the most appropriate. As had been pointed out in the Court of Appeal, there was a clear need to develop a comprehensive method of handling such cases and the Divisional Court had particular expertise in the area.

It was suggested that there were three circumstances where the JRP might be inappropriate:
- where the matter was collateral to another application (applied in *Cocks v Thanet DC* (HL, 1982));
- where public law issues are raised as a defence to criminal charges (see *Wandsworth LBC v Winder* (CA, 1985));
- otherwise on a case-to-case basis. It may be inappropriate to use the JRP in a complex Chancery matter for example, or other instance where the procedure is inappropriate (*D v The Home Office* (CA, 2006)).

Subsequent cases led to concern that the existence of a public law element, however slight, was forcing litigants to use the JRP and deprive them of the right to bring an action for private law relief. *Roy v Kensington & Chelsea & Westminster Family Practitioner Committee* (HL, 1992) represented a retreat from this exclusivity principle. The House of Lords identified two approaches:
- a broad approach under which Order 53 would only be insisted on if private rights were not in issue;
- a narrow approach which required applicants to proceed by the JRP in all proceedings in which public law matters are challenged subject to those exceptions already noted.

It followed the broad approach and found the fact that there was an incidental public law matter did not prevent the litigant from seeking to establish his right by action. This approach has been confirmed by the House of Lords in *R. v Secretary of State for Employment Ex p. EOC* (HL, 1994) and *Mercury Communications Ltd v Director General of Telecommunications* (HL, 1996) and in *Clark v University of Lincolnshire and Humberside* (CA, 2000) where the court was not willing to strike out a claim simply because it might have been more appropriate to bring it by way of judicial review. Lord Woolf identified as the crucial factor the question of whether the protections afforded by the JRP had been flouted in circumstances which were inconsistent with the general principles contained in the CPR Pt 1.

NON-JUDICIAL REMEDIES

The individual who has a complaint against the administration may chose to use a non-judicial route. He may ask his MP to raise the matter with the minister, e.g. through a written or oral question in Parliament (see Ch.4). This allows discussion of the merits of the decision in a way not available in judicial review. He may approach one of the Commissioners for Administration and request that the matter be investigated. This allows a consideration of whether there has been maladministration, a term which covers a range of situations much wider than those which give rise to judicial review.

The Parliamentary Commissioner

Following considerable pressure to establish a mechanism to investigate complaints by members of the public who felt that they had suffered injustice at the hands of central government, the Parliamentary Commissioner Act 1967 was passed providing for the appointment of a Commissioner to investigate complaints of maladministration by those government bodies and public authorities listed in the Act. This list includes government departments such as the Home Office and the Inland Revenue, but also non-departmental bodies such as the Arts Council. He cannot look into the activities of the police, the nationalised industries, the Cabinet Office or local government departments (a separate Local Government Commission was established under the Local Government Act 1974).

Maladministration is not defined in the Act however, it has been defined as "any kind of administrative shortcoming, poor administration or the wrong application of rules". Richard Crossman, speaking during the Second Reading debate on the passage of the Bill through the Commons said, in what has become known as the "Crossman Catalogue", that maladministration might include "bias, neglect, inattention, delay, incompetence, ineptitude, perversity, turpitude, arbitrariness and so on". In *R. v Local Commissioner for Administration North East England Ex p. Bradford MCC* (CA, 1979), a case involving the jurisdiction of the Local Commission which has similar terms of reference, Lord Denning accepted the Crossman Catalogue as an adequate description of the scope of the term.

The following have been found to constitute maladministration:
- failure to provide necessary information and advice;
- failure to provide an adequate explanation;

- provision of inadequate or misleading information and advice;
- basing decision on false or inadequate information, ignoring relevant evidence;
- avoidable delay;
- faulty procedures or failure to follow departmental rules and procedures;
- rudeness and inconsiderate behaviour by officials;
- bias or prejudice;
- failure to monitor faulty procedures, e.g. DTI monitoring of Barlow Clowes.

Despite the broad interpretation of maladministration, several exclusions apply:

1. section 12(3) of the Act expressly excludes consideration of the merits of the decision;
2. the PC will not normally investigate a matter for which the complainant has a legal remedy before the courts unless there is doubt about its availability or to pursue the remedy would be slow or expensive;
3. the PC can only investigate the exercise of administrative functions. He cannot investigate judicial or legislative (s.12(3));
4. he has refused to investigate matters which he considers to be purely political, e.g. the allocation of time between political parties for party political broadcasts;
5. the PC is excluded from considering those matters listed in the Third Schedule of the Act. These include:
   (a) actions affecting relations with other governments or international organisations;
   (b) actions taken under the Extradition Act 1989 or the Fugitive Offenders Act 1967;
   (c) administration of territories overseas;
   (d) security and passport matters, criminal investigations;
   (e) commencement or conduct of legal proceedings;
   (f) the exercise of the prerogative of mercy;
   (g) actions taken in relation to contractual or other commercial transactions excluding certain matters relating to compulsory purchase;
   (h) personnel matters relating to those bodies covered by the Act;
   (i) the grant of honours, awards and privileges within the gift of the Crown.

Restrictions (g) and (h) have been widely criticised.

Investigation of complaints

Complaints to the PC are confidential and his investigations are private. The service is free. Complaints must be channelled through MPs not necessarily the complainant's own (*R. v Parliamentary Commissioner for Administration Ex p. Atholl Grant Murray* (CA, 2002)). If the PC decides to conduct an investigation, he must, under s.7(1), give the department concerned the opportunity of commenting on any allegations made. There are wide powers of investigation, a right to question ministers and civil servants, a right to look at all necessary documents. The right to go into the department in question and examine files is of considerable value. He is denied access only to Cabinet Papers, a restriction which the PC has said is no real practical hindrance. The duty to assist him overrides any obligation to maintain secrecy under the **Official Secrets Acts**. Under s.11, the minister can give the PC notice that the publication of certain information would be prejudicial to the interests of the State. The minister cannot, however, veto the investigation.

The case of *R. v Parliamentary Commissioner for Administration Ex p. Dyer* (DC, 1994) illustrates the reluctance of the courts to review the way the PC carries out his functions. Only in extreme cases of abuse of power might they intervene. They were, in general, unwilling to interfere with the exercise of his discretion.

The result of the investigation

When the report is completed, the PC sends a report to the MP, the department investigated and any other person concerned. If indeed maladministration has been established, the report will suggest what action might be taken to remedy it. Sometimes this may be a financial payment, sometimes that a decision be reversed, sometimes an apology. (See, for example, the ex gratia payments made by the Government following the Commissioner's Report on the Barlow Clowes case and payments made by the Inland Revenue following late payments as a result of problems with a new computer system at the Contributions Agency.)

The PC does not have any direct sanction and he cannot enforce his recommendations. Under s.10(3) he may, however, lay a special report before Parliament. On occasions the Government may choose to ignore the recommendations as, for example, in 2006 over the PC's findings that the Government had given misleading advice to people considering transferring from state to private pension schemes. As well as suggesting a remedy for the individual complainant, the PC is equally concerned to suggest administrative changes which would prevent the occurrence of maladministration in the future. The PC must make an annual report to Parliament and his work is monitored by the House of Commons Public Administration Select Committee.

In addition to the Parliamentary Commissioner for Administration, there are now a separate Scottish Parliamentary Commissioner and Welsh Administration Ombudsman, Health Service Commissioners for England, Wales and Scotland, Local Government Commissioners for England, Wales and Scotland, an Information Commissioner, a Legal Services Commissioner, and a European Union and Community Ombudsman. Indeed the idea has also been adopted in the private sector, for example in banking.

SUMMARY

When assessing a claim for judicial review, the following questions should be asked:

- Is the decision made by a body exercising a public law function?

- Does the applicant have standing?

- Has the applicant complied with the time limit?

- Has the applicant complied with the pre-action protocol?

- Are any of the grounds for judicial review present? (See Ch.8)

- Is the applicant seeking one of the available remedies?

Revision checklist

You should now know and understand:

- the scope of judicial review, including who has standing to apply for judicial review;
- the types of decisions which may be challenged by means of judicial review;
- the remedies which are available to the court in judicial review cases;
- the procedure for challenging the decisions of bodies exercising public law functions.

QUESTION AND ANSWER

The Question

The requirements of standing in judicial review cases are excessively liberal, draining the resources of our public bodies and wasting court time.

Discuss.

Advice and the Answer

General guidance

This question requires the student to display an understanding of the rules of standing in judicial review claims. However, it also requires a critical analysis of the rules, particularly whether an argument could be made that the interests of justice would be better served by a tightening of the rules of standing in judicial review cases.

Points of answer

- An individual applying for judicial review must have sufficient interest in the matter to which the application relates (s.31(3) **Supreme Court Act 1981**).
- No statutory definition of what constitutes a "sufficient interest".
- *R. v IRC Ex p. The National Federation of Self Employed and Small Businesses Ltd* (HL, 1982) is the key case on the issue of standing in judicial review cases and should be discussed in some detail.

- It was held that in this case that standing would be considered in two stages:
  - filter stage;
  - substantive hearing.
- The court also held that the applicants' standing should be considered in the context of the merits of the case, providing evidence of a link between the rules of standing and the seriousness of the illegality complained of.
- The test for standing has been liberally applied in the intervening years. Examples of the types of individuals and groups which have passed the sufficient interest test include:
  - business competitors (*R. v Department of Transport Ex p. Presvac Engineering Ltd* (CA, 1991));
  - those with "legitimate expectation that they will be heard" (*O'Reilly v Mackman* (HL, 1983));
  - pressure groups (*R. v HM Inspectorate of Pollution Ex p. Greenpeace* (DC, 1994));
  - claimants with "a sincere concern" for constitutional issues (*R. v Secretary of State for Foreign and Commonwealth Affairs Ex p. Rees-Mogg* (HC, 1994);
  - claimants who raised issues which were of such a nature that it was in the public interest that the matters raised were considered by the court and no other challenger was likely (*R. v Secretary of State for Foreign Affairs Ex p. World Development Movement* (HL, 1995)—WDM was reputable body with expertise).
- Note, if an application for judicial review indicates a breach of human rights, s.7 requires that the applicant be a "victim".

The Basis of Intervention

8

INTRODUCTION

The process of judicial review involves a review of the legality of decisions made by bodies exercising public law functions and the courts may review the legality of these decisions on several different grounds.

The principal grounds for review of a decision as identified by Lord Diplock in *CCSU v The Minister for the Civil Service* (HL, 1984) are:
- illegality;
- irrationality;
- procedural impropriety.

Note that proportionality was also identified as an emerging ground for review.

It should be noted that while these headings are useful, there is considerable overlap between the grounds. In *Boddington v British Transport Police* (HL, 1998), Lord Irvine of Lairg noted that:

> "[c]ategorisation of types of challenge assists in an orderly exposition of the principles underlying our developing public law. But these are not water tight compartments because the various grounds for judicial review run together."

This chapter will consider the following:
- illegality as a grounds for challenging decisions made by bodies exercising public law functions, including the ways in which such illegality may occur;
- the test of irrationality in judicial review proceedings;
- procedural impropriety, both express and implied, as a ground for review;
- whether proportionality could be considered to be a separate ground for review.

GROUNDS FOR REVIEW

Illegality

> "By illegality as a ground for judicial review I mean that the decision maker must understand correctly the law that regulates his decision making power and must give effect to it."
>
> Per Lord Diplock in *CCSU v The Minister for the Civil Service* (HL, 1984)

This illegality might occur in a number of ways, including:

- mistakes of jurisdiction—for example, misinterpreting power or factual mistakes;
- abuse of discretion—for example, taking into account irrelevant considerations;
- failure to exercise discretion—for example, unlawful delegation;
- acting contrary to s.6 **HRA**.

Mistakes of Jurisdiction

A decision will be considered to be ultra vires or illegal if the decision maker acts beyond the power given to him/her by statute. In *Att-Gen v Fulham Corp* (HC, 1921) the local authority had power under the **Baths and Wash Houses Acts 1846–1878** to establish baths, wash houses and open bathing places. The court held that this did not give it the power to operate a commercial laundry.

To determine the legality of the action or decision the court must determine the area over which power is given. In *Commissioners of Customs and Excise v Cure & Deeley* (HC, 1961), Sachs J. said that in carrying out its task, the court was bound to examine "the nature, the objects and scheme of the parent act, and in the light of that examination, to consider what is the area over which power is given". If the scope of a body's power is uncertain as the statute is unclear, the court will rely on presumptions of statutory interpretation to assist them, such as the presumption that a body has no power to act retrospectively and the presumption that a body has no power to restrict a person's access to the courts. (*Chester v Bateson* (HC, 1920) and *R. v Lord Chancellor Ex p. Witham* (DC, 1997).) Cases such as *Bromley LBC v GLC* (HL, 1982) demonstrate that determining the scope of a body's power is far from being a mechanical task but involves the court in making value judgments. Any exercise of power by the authority which falls outside that area will be invalid.

The courts will also review decisions to determine whether there has been an error of fact (*S of S for Education and Science v Tameside MBC* (HL, 1977)) or law (*Anisminic Ltd v Foreign Compensation Commission* (HL,1969)). However, the court are more willing to review errors of law than errors of fact as often the body making the decision will be in a better position than the court to evaluate and apply the facts, having all the expertise and factual information available to them. There is a danger that a review of whether a body has made its decision on the basis of an error of fact may result in a blurring of the separation of powers (*R (on app of Iran) v S of S for Home Dept* (CA, 2005)). For this reason, the courts limit reviews on the basis of errors of fact to facts which impact upon the decision maker's power to make a particular decision.

Abuse of discretion

Public bodies need wide discretion to exercise their public law duties, however, this discretion is not unlimited.

A body will be deemed to be acting illegally if it:
- takes into account irrelevant factors when making a decision;
- does not consider factors which are relevant;
- makes a decision for purposes not connected to the power.

In *Padfield v Minister of Agriculture, Fisheries and Food* (HL, 1968) the minister had the power to refer complaints about the operation of the Milk Marketing Board scheme to a committee. He refused to refer a complaint of substance to the committee. Padfield contended that the Minister had allowed wider political motivations to influence his decisions and it subsequently emerged that he had taken into account the fact that publicity about the complaint would be politically damaging for the Government at that time. This, the court said, was an irrelevant consideration which rendered his decision unlawful. Lord Upjohn said that unlawful behaviour might be constituted by:
- an outright refusal to consider the relevant matter;
- a misdirection on a point of law;
- taking into account some wholly irrelevant or extraneous consideration;
- wholly omitting to take into account a relevant consideration.

Lord Reid noted that:

> "if the Minister uses his discretion as to thwart or run contrary to the policy and objects of the Act, then our law would be very

defective if persons aggrieved were not entitled to the protection
of the court".

In *R. v Somerset CC Ex p. Fewings* (CA, 1995), a local authority decision to ban
stag hunting on its land was quashed. Under its statutory power it was
required to take an objective judgment about the proper management of its
land. Clearly the ban was imposed because hunting was seen as being
morally repulsive. Such ethical considerations were held to be irrelevant in
terms of the local authority's powers to manage the land.

Essentially the court is concerned whether the decision-making body
has addressed itself to all relevant factors. It is not concerned with the
question of whether proper weight has been given to those factors (*Pickwell v
Camden LBC* (HC, 1983)). But where the decision is reached on the basis of
two quite separate considerations, one which is relevant and one which the
authority is not entitled to take into account, the court must decide which
was the dominant consideration. If this is an irrelevant consideration then the
authority's action will be reviewable (*R. v ILEA Ex p. Westminster Council* (HC,
1986)).

An example of improper use of powers occurred in *R. v Secretary of
State for Foreign Affairs Ex p. The World Development Movement Ltd* (HL,
1995) where the payment of overseas aid to fund the construction of the
Pergau Dam in Malaysia was held to be illegal as it was made for a purpose
not envisaged by the relevant statute. Similarly, in Padfield's case, discussed
above, Lord Reid pointed out that Parliament had given the minister discretion as to whether complaints were referred to the committee. It was not,
however, an unlimited discretion. He argued that it could be implied that it
had been given with the intention that it should be used to promote the
policy and objects of the enabling Act.

One difficulty is how the courts ascertain the policy of any Act of
Parliament. Rarely is this expressed in the statute. In *Padfield*, Lord Reid said
that the courts must carry out this task by construing the Act as a whole.
Sometimes it is impossible to determine the purpose and no intervention is
possible on this ground as, for example, in *British Oxygen Co Ltd v Minister of
Technology* (HL, 1971). On the other hand, in *Congrieve v The Home Office* (CA,
1976) the minister had a statutory power under the Wireless Telegraphy Act
1949 to revoke television licences. He used this apparently unrestricted
power to revoke licences purchased early to avoid an increase. The court held
that the minister had acted ultra vires in that he had used his power for an
improper purpose. Lord Denning said that it could be implied that the minister had been given this power only to enable him to revoke licences
obtained illegally.

The decision in *Pepper v Hart* (HL, 1993) now makes it possible for the courts to look at Hansard in attempting to ascertain the purpose for which power was given.

Failure to exercise discretion

A failure to exercise discretion by the decision maker may also result in a decision being deemed illegal. For example, a statute might prescribe that the power should be exercised by a named person or a person with specific qualifications and if the power is exercised by another it may be an ultra vires act which is a nullity. Thus, where power is exercised by someone who does not meet the qualifications laid down in the grant of power, the act may be considered illegal. In *Allingham v The Minister of Agriculture and Fisheries* (HC, 1948), the minister had a statutory power to give directions regarding the cultivation of land for agricultural purposes. He had an express power to delegate this function to a committee which, in turn, attempted to further sub-delegate its functions to an executive officer who issued a directive to a farmer that only sugar should be grown in a particular field. The farmer failed to comply with the direction and, when fined, challenged its validity alleging that the executive officer had no power to issue it. The court quashed the conviction finding that only the minister or the committee had the power to issue such orders under the statute. In *R. v DPP Ex p. Association of First Division Civil Servants* (DC, 1988) the delegation of certain functions under the Prosecution of Offences Act to non-lawyers was held to be unlawful.

However, it must be remembered that the courts will sometimes imply a power to sub-delegate into a statutory provision. In *Vine v The National Dock Labour Board* (HL, 1957), Lord Somervell of Harrow said that in deciding whether there is such a power, two factors have to be considered:

- the nature of the power;
- the character of the person.

If the power is of a routine nature the courts will be more willing to imply a power to sub-delegate than if there is a strong element of discretion involved. They have also shown themselves reluctant to allow any sub-delegation of judicial or legislative powers. If the body exercising the power has been established especially for that purpose, the courts are likely to conclude that Parliament intended the body to act personally. Where the power is exercised by a minister, for practical reasons, the courts are more willing to hold that he has an implied power to sub-delegate (*Carltona v Commissioner of Works* (CA, 1943)). It should be noted, however, that often when a minister acts through his civil servants, there is no delegation. The civil servant is simply acting as the alter ego of the minister (*R. v Secretary of State for the Home Office Ex p. Oladehinde* (HL, 1990)).

Acting contrary to s.6 HRA

A new sub-ground of judicial review has been created by virtue of the **Human Rights Act** 1998. Section 6 makes it unlawful for a Public Authority to act incompatibly with an individual's convention rights and the courts will review decisions or actions of bodies exercising public functions on this basis.

Figure 8.1: Illegality

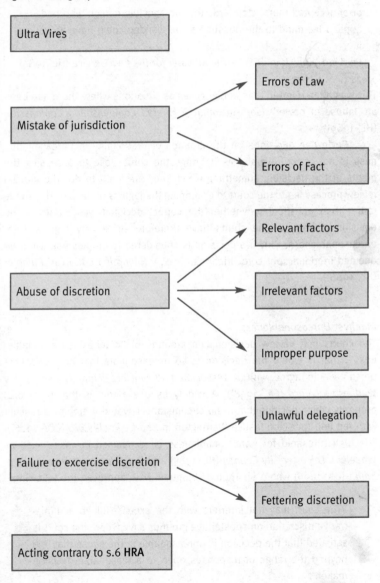

Irrationality

Irrationality is the second ground on which Lord Diplock would exercise the powers of review.

> **DEFINITION CHECKPOINT**
>
> Irrationality
>
> "[i]t applies to a decision which is so outrageous in its defiance of logic or of accepted moral standards that no sensible person who had applied his mind to the question to be decided could have arrived at it."
>
> Per Lord Diplock in *CCSU v The Minister for the Civil Service* (HL, 1984)

This was often referred to in earlier cases as situations where there had been an "abuse of power" (see *Anisminic v Foreign Compensation Commission* (HL, 1969)).

Reviewing decisions on the grounds of irrationality or unreasonableness is not uncontroversial as it brings the court close to assessing the merits of the decision, something which they are loath to do. The judicial review process limits the court to examining the legality of the decision made rather than questioning whether the correct decision was made by the decision maker and the courts have therefore set a very high test for unreasonableness. Only if a decision is considered to be perverse will it be deemed irrational (per Lord Brightman in *R. v Hillingdon LBC Ex p. Pulhofer* (HL, 1986)).

Manifest Unreasonableness

The courts may review decisions on grounds of "manifest unreasonableness", that is where the decision is so unreasonable that no reasonable person would agree with it (*Associated Provincial Picture Houses Ltd v Wednesbury Corp* (CA, 1948)). A widely used example is that of a local authority which decides that in no circumstances would it employ a teacher with red hair (per Lord Justice Warrington in *Short v Poole Corp* (COA,1926)). The high threshold for unreasonableness is recognised in cases such as *Wheeler v Leicester City Council* (HL, 1985) and *R. v Ministry of Defence Ex p. Smith* (CA, 1996) where Sir Thomas Bingham M.R. approved the following:

> "The court may not interfere with the exercise of an administrative discretion on substantive grounds save where the court is satisfied that the decision is unreasonable in the sense that it is beyond the range of responses open to a reasonable decision maker."

Henry L.J. in *R. v Lord Chancellor Ex p. Maxwell* (CA, 1996) described a very high standard of unreasonableness, "decisions so unreasonable as to warrant interference jump off the page at you".

When considering whether a decision is irrational, the court may look to at some of issues outlined above (whether there has been an abuse of discretion) as evidence of irrationality. So for example, if a body acting under statutory authority takes an irrelevant consideration, into account or ignores a relevant consideration this will be taken as evidence of unreasonableness and the resultant decision will be open to challenge on the grounds of both illegality (see above) or irrationality (*Associated Provincial Picture Houses Ltd v Wednesbury Corp* (CA, 1948)). Similarly, the courts have held that if a public body exercises its statutory power for an improper purpose this may provide evidence of irrationality.

Failure to give reasons

One effect of a failure to give reasons for a decision is that it may suggest that there is no good reason and that the resultant decision is irrational. Unreasonableness will not always be inferred from the absence of reasons (*Lonrho Plc v Secretary of State* (HL, 1989)) but in *Padfield* (above), Lord Pearce clearly felt that it gave rise to the possibility. Failure to give reasons may also constitute procedural impropriety (see below).

Beyond Wednesbury unreasonableness

Article 13 of the ECHR requires subscribing states to provide an effective remedy to those claiming their rights have been infringed. In cases such as *Smith and Grady v UK* (ECHR, 1999), the European Court of Human Rights has found that judicial review on grounds of "Wednesbury unreasonableness" did not provide an effective remedy. This is despite the fact that in cases involving interference with convention rights, the English courts have indicated that they would give the issue "anxious or heightened scrutiny" and adopt a lower threshold of unreasonableness than that normally applied. (See *R. v Ministry of Defence Ex p. Smith* (CA, 1996) and *R. v Lord Saville of Newdigate Ex p. A* (CA, 1999).)

In *R. (Mahmood) v The Home Secretary* (CA, 2001), the Court of Appeal considered the proper standard for intervention on grounds of unreasonableness and Lord Justice Laws emphasised that the courts should not consider the merits of the decision for then they would be acting as a court of appeal. Whether they adopted the lower threshold as expounded in *Smith* or the more stringent approach in *Wednesbury* depended on the subject matter of the dispute. However, in cases involving conventions rights it would seem that the court would have to come close to looking at the merits of the decision to satisfy the ECHR.

The passage of the **Human Rights Act 1998** which incorporates Con-
on rights into domestic law, has led to further developments in this area.
. v The Home Secretary Ex p. Daly (HL, 2001), Lord Steyn felt that the test
unreasonableness needed to be further developed. He felt that neither the
pproach in *Wednesbury* nor that in *Smith* provided adequate protection for
:onvention rights. He suggested that the court, in deciding whether a decision was unreasonable, might consider whether it was proportionate. In *Huan*
v Home Secretary (HL, 2007), the court felt that Lord Steyn wished to make
clear that, although the convention calls for a more exacting standard of
review, it remains that the judge is not the primary decision maker.

Proportionality

While the importance of the doctrine of proportionality in cases involving
fundamental rights has been highlighted, in the *CCSU* case Lord Diplock had
suggested that the principle of "proportionality" might develop into a ground
of judicial review in English law applicable in all cases. The doctrine of
proportionality has long been part of the jurisprudence of the ECJ and the
ECHR and is concerned with questions of balance and whether the means
justify the ends:

> "An appropriate balance must be maintained between the
> adverse effects which an administrative authority's decision may
> have on the rights, liberties or interests of the person concerned
> and the purpose which the authority is seeking to pursue."
> (Committee of Ministers of the Council of Europe in 1980).

In *de Freitas v Permanent Secretary of Ministry of Agriculture, Fisheries, Lands
and Housing* (PC, 1999), the court said the question to be asked was:

> "whether the legislative objective was sufficiently important to
> justify limiting a fundamental right; whether the measures
> designed to meet the legislative objective are rationally con-
> nected to it and whether the means used to impair the right or
> freedom are no more than is necessary to accomplish the
> objective".

Proportionality as a ground of challenge was recognised by Lord Slynn of
Hadley in the *Alconbury* case *(R. (Alconbury Developments Ltd) v Secretary of
State for Transport, Environment and the Regions* (HL, 2001)) when he said, "I
consider that ... the time has come to recognise that this principle [pro-
portionality] ... is part of English administrative law, ... even when dealing
with acts under domestic law."

doctrine of proportionality may require the reviewing court to
asse balance which the decision maker has struck, not merely whether
it is the range of rational or reasonable decisions. As such it may go
furth the traditional grounds of review as it may require attention to be
direc the relative weight to be attached to the various factors involved.
In A*on of British Civilian Internees, Far Eastern Region v Secretary of
State*fence (CA, 2003), it was noted that proportionality and Wednes-
bur*onableness did not always yield the same result. Yet Lord Steyn in
*Daly*t proportionality added little to the concept of unreasonableness.
If th, it is difficult to see how the courts have satisfied the vigorous
revi*nded by the ECHR.

Pro impropriety

The und of judicial review requires the court to assess whether the
dec*er has complied with all procedural requirements. Procedural
imp*ncompasses breaches of both express requirements laid down
by *d implied procedural requirements, such as the requirement to
com*he rules of natural justice.

Bre*ress procedural requirement

The* review a decision where there has been a failure to comply
wit*rocedural requirements contained in an Act of Parliament or
sec*slation such as consultation requirements or the need to hold
inq

ct of non-compliance with a procedural requirement varies,
de* its importance. Traditionally, the courts have categorised
req*s either mandatory or directory. Only where the breach is
co*e of a mandatory procedural requirement will non-compliance
aff*ty of the exercise of power as in *Agricultural Training Board v
Ay*rooms* (HC, 1972). Breach of a directory requirement will not
aff*. *v Sheer Metalcraft Ltd* (HC, 1948)).

ss of determining whether a particular procedural require-
m*ry or directory is one of statutory interpretation. What does
Pa*d to be the result of the breach? Of course, Parliament rarely
pr* guidance and the court must assess the importance of the
re* its relationship to the general purpose of the statutory
fra*ich it is set. (Lord Penzance in *Howard v Bodington* (HL,
18

London & Clydeside Estates Ltd v Aberdeen DC (HL, 1980),
Lo*riticised a too rigid distinction between mandatory and
di*al requirements. Not only was it often difficult to ascertain
Pa*tion but the significance of a breach might vary with the

circumstances of each case. He said that the court was faced with a spm of possibilities. At one end there were serious procedural defectsh would render any decision a nullity. Other defects were so trivial as 'e no effect. But in the middle, cases would arise where the courts o exercise their discretion, cases where differences of degree merged t imperceptibly into differences of kind.

Thus in *Secretary of State for Trade and Industry v Langridge* (CA, Balcombe L.J. considered the following in determining the effect · compliance with a procedural requirement:

- the importance of the relevant procedural requirement;
- the relation of that requirement to the general object intende secured by the Act; and
- the relevant circumstances of the case.

Lord Woolf in *R. v The Home Secretary, Ex p. Jeyeanthan* (1999) sugges the court must also consider whether substantial compliance would f requisite procedural requirements and whether non-compliance was of being waived.

Breach of implied procedural requirements

The courts have often implied procedural requirements such as cons a requirement to give reasons and the duty to follow a fair proced implication is usually drawn from a previous course of dealing betv parties giving rise to a legitimate expectation that the procedure will followed. For example, in the *CCSU* case, the unions had been con the past about proposed changes to terms and conditions of em and this gave rise to a legitimate expectation that they would consulted. The implication may also be drawn from the fact that as have been given e.g. that there will be consultation (*R. (Montp Trevors Association v City of Westminster* (HC, 2005)).

Where consultation is required, a failure to carry it out proper to invalidate the decision (*Agricultural Training Board v Aylesb rooms* (HC, 1972)). The consultation must involve a genuine invitat advice and a willingness to listen to the advice with a receptive ficient information must be given to enable those consulted to re they must be given sufficient time to do so (*R. v Secretary of S Environment Ex p. Association of Metropolitan Authorities* (HC, 19

Implied requirements of fairness

Historically, the concept of fairness was tied up with the rule justice which were traditionally applied to judicial decisions.

There were two aspects to the rule of natural justice:
1. The Nemo Judex rule—no man should be a judge in his own cause.
2. The Audi Alteram Partem rule—the right to a fair hearing.

For much of the twentieth century the courts restricted natural justice to judicial decisions taken by court like bodies. The case of *Ridge v Baldwin* (HL, 1964) opened up the application of the rules of natural justice to a much wider range of circumstances. The Chief Constable of Brighton was dismissed from office by the Brighton Watch Committee without an adequate hearing. Did the rules of natural justice apply? The decision clearly affected the Chief Constable's legal rights, including his pension rights. It could, however, be argued that the Watch Committee was acting in an executive or administrative capacity rather than judicially and was therefore not subject to the rules of natural justice. Lord Reid, however, greatly extended the scope of natural justice by requiring the Watch Committee to give the Chief Constable a fair hearing, arguing that justice demanded it.

This principle has been recognised in subsequent judicial decisions. In the *CCSU* case, for example, Lord Scarman indicated there was an implied duty of fairness attached to all administrative acts. In *Doody v The Home Secretary* (HL, 1993), Lord Mustill said that where an Act of Parliament confers an administrative power there is a presumption that it will be exercised in a manner which is fair.

The requirement of Art.6 of the ECHR that "in the determination of his civil rights and obligations or of any criminal charge against him, everyone is entitled to a fair and public hearing within a reasonable time by an independent and impartial tribunal", imposes a further requirement of fair decision making.

What standard of fairness will be required will vary depending on the type of decision, who takes it and the circumstances (see Lord Mustill in *Doody*) but, in general, judicial decisions, decisions which involve allegations being considered or decisions the result of which will have serious consequences for the individual will attract the most stringent requirements.

Right to a fair hearing
The courts will imply a right to a hearing before the decision maker in certain circumstances. In *McInnes v Onslow Fane* (HC, 1978), for example, a contrast was drawn between cases involving forfeiture of a licence, renewal cases and initial applications. In the first two instances there was a legitimate expectation of being granted a hearing but not in the case of an initial application where minimal standards of fairness applied. But where an initial application would only be refused because of allegations against the applicant for

example, justice might require he be given a hearing to answer any such allegations. The courts have, in fact, adopted a pragmatic approach to determining whether a hearing need be given. In recent years, circumstances where it has been refused have variously related to a feeling that a hearing would serve no useful purpose, would be impractical in the circumstances, would have no effect on the outcome or where it should be excluded for security reasons (see *Cinnamond v British Airport Authority* (CA, 1980)).

Where a hearing is necessary, the minimum requirement is that the person must have an adequate opportunity of presenting his case (*Local Government Board v Arlidge* (HL, 1915)). This does not mean that a person is always entitled to an oral hearing (*R. v Criminal Injuries Compensation Board Ex p. Dickson* (CA, 1996)) and (*R. (on the application of Heather Moor & Edgecomb) v Financial Ombudsman Service* (HC, 2009)). In *SP v Secretary of State for the Home Department* (HC, 2004), fairness required that a prisoner should be allowed to make representations before he was segregated within a young offenders' institution unless, in the circumstances, it would be contrary to good order and discipline to allow him that right.

The courts are concerned to see that there is equality of treatment between the parties. So, for example, the rule was broken when the court heard one side in the absence of the other (*Errington v Minister of Health* (CA, 1935)). In *R. v National Lottery Commission Ex p. Camelot Group Plc* (HC, 2000), the court quashed the decision of the Lottery Commission to exclude Camelot from further negotiations on lottery rights. It said that the procedure had been conspicuously unfair as a result of "a marked lack of even-handedness between the parties".

A person must also have adequate notice of any charges to be brought against him or any matters that have to be taken into account (*Kanda v Government of Malaya* (PC, 1962)). The court said:

> "If the right to be heard is a real right which is worth anything, it must carry with it a right in the accused man to know the case which is made against him. He must know what evidence has been given and what statements have been made affecting him, and then he must be given a fair opportunity to correct or contradict them."

In *R. v Secretary of State for the Home Department Ex p. Georghiades* (DC, 1992), the court said that justice and fairness required that a prisoner should be told why his parole licence had been revoked to enable him to present his case to the Parole Board.

A person must also have a reasonable time to prepare his case. In *R. v*

Thames Magistrates Ex p. Polemis (HC, 1974) the court held that if a person had been given insufficient time, an adjournment must be granted.

The tribunal need not always observe the strict procedures of a court of justice. In *R. v Commissioner for Racial Equality Ex p. Cottrell* (HC, 1980), it was said that as the function being exercised was more administrative than judicial, the attendance and cross-examination of witnesses, from whom statements had been taken, at a formal hearing was unnecessary. Contrast this with *R. v Board of Visitors of Hull Prison Ex p. St Germain No.2* (HC, 1979) where it was said that persons charged with serious disciplinary offences had a right to call any evidence which was likely to assist in establishing vital facts in issue, and that the chairman had a discretion to refuse to call witnesses to prevent the accused calling so many witnesses as to make the system unworkable but that fairness demanded that there be a right to cross-examine witnesses.

The courts do not appear to consider that legal assistance is an absolute requirement of the rule although there is a readiness to imply it if procedural rules are silent. Legal assistance may not necessarily involve legal representation as an oral hearing is not always necessary.

A long standing principle in administrative law has been that tribunals should develop appropriate procedures and these are not necessarily modelled on court-like procedures. Legal representation may have the effect of formalising the procedure where the aim is to make the decision maker approachable and informal. So should the courts interfere where a tribunal makes a rule preventing legal representation? Lord Denning has gone further than any other judge in demonstrating a willingness to require legal representation even where this is prohibited by the procedural rules governing the body in question (see, e.g. *Pett v Greyhound Racing Association* (CA, 1969)). His views were criticised by the House of Lords, for example in *Pett No. 2* (HL, 1970) and even he held in *Maynard v Osmond* (CA, 1977) that legal representation was not an absolute requirement where a police officer who was facing disciplinary charges was denied legal representation under the Police Disciplinary Regulations. The officer was, however, entitled to assistance from another officer.

R. v Board of Visitors of Wormwood Scrubs Prison Ex p. Anderson (HC, 1983) held that the Board of Visitors should have exercised its discretion to allow legal representation in view of the seriousness of the charges and the potential penalty, the need for fairness between the parties involved and the ability of the prisoners to represent themselves. Other relevant factors might be the complexity of the case and whether any points of law were likely to arise. See also *R. v Board of Visitors of HM Prison, The Maze Ex p. Hone* (HL, 1988).

Article 6(3)(a) of the ECHR provides that everyone charged with a criminal offence has a right to defend himself through legal assistance.

The duty to give reasons
One particular requirement of fairness might be a duty to give reasons in support of a decision. In *R. v Higher Education Funding Council Ex p. Institute of Dental Surgery* (CA, 1994), it was held that there was no general duty to give reasons but it depended on the individual circumstances. Factors identified as relevant as to whether such a duty would be implied were:
- where the decision involved an interest which was highly regarded in law such as personal liberty (see *R. v Ministry of Defence Ex p. Murray* (DC, 1997));
- where the nature of the process required reasons to be given (see *R. v Secretary of State Ex p. Doody* (HL, 1994));
- from the circumstances of the individual case (see *R. v Civil Service Appeal Board Ex p. Cunningham* (CA, 1992)).

It is now clear that where the decision constitutes a determination which affects an individual's civil rights and obligations, Art.6(10) of the ECHR requires the decision maker to give a reasoned judgment.

The rule against bias
The right to be heard by an unbiased judge arises both out of common law and as a result of Art.6(1) of the ECHR.

If the judge has a pecuniary interest in the outcome of a case then he is absolutely barred from hearing it. There is no need to show actual bias. The mere existence of the interest is sufficient to disqualify the judge (*Dimes v Grand Junction Canal* (HL, 1852)). A direct pecuniary or proprietary interest, however small, is conclusively presumed to create a real danger of bias (per Sedley J. in *R. v Secretary of State for the Environment Ex p. Kirkstall Valley Campaign Ltd* (DC, 1996)). The interest must not, however, be too remote (*R. v Rand* (HC, 1866)).

This automatic disqualification was extended in *R. v Bow Street Magistrates Ex p. Pinochet* (HL, 1999), beyond a pecuniary or direct proprietary interest in the case to where the judge himself is a party to or has relevant interests in the case in question. The judge had an involvement with Amnesty which had presented evidence in the case. Lord Browne-Wilkinson said that in such a case "[the judge] is disqualified without any investigation as to whether there was a likelihood or suspicion of bias". Other situations where bias may arise include as a result of family relationships (*Metropolitan Properties v Lannon* (CA, 1969)); and business connection (*R. v Sussex Justices Ex p. McCarthy* (HC, 1924)).

Disqualification may also arise where the circumstances surrounding the case suggest in some way that the judge was biased. Perhaps it appeared that he had already made up his mind before taking the decision. In *Ex p. Hook* (CA, 1976), for example, it was clearly wrong that the person making the allegations against the market-trader should participate in the decision as to whether he should lose his licence as he would be acting both as a prosecutor and as a judge. As the court said in Locabail, "It would be dangerous and futile to attempt to define or list the factors which may give rise to a real danger of bias. Everything will depend on the facts". In such cases, while it is not necessary to establish actual bias, it is necessary to show that the decision has given the appearance of bias. In *R. v Sussex Justices, Ex p. McCarthy* (HC, 1924) the court said that "it is of fundamental importance that justice should not only be done but should manifestly and undoubtedly be seen to be done."

How is the test of bias formulated? In *R. v Gough* (HL, 1994) the House of Lords formulated the following test: was there a real danger of injustice occurring as a result of the alleged bias—a real possibility rather than the probability of bias.

In *Re Medicaments and Related Classes of Goods (No.2)* (CA, 2001), the court reviewed the Gough test to ensure it was in line with convention requirements and the approach taken by the ECHR. It felt that, in general, the two approaches coincided, subject to a modest adjustment to the Gough test to emphasise that the court was applying an objective test in the circumstances and not making a judgment on the likelihood of a particular tribunal being, in fact, biased. Lord Steyn in *Porter v McGill* (HL, 2001) summed up the position by saying that "the question is whether the fair minded and informed observer, having considered the facts, would conclude that there was a real danger of bias."

The effect of the **Human Rights Act** is that where Art.6(1) applies, there is a right to an independent and impartial tribunal. The ECHR in *Findlay v UK* (1997) said that in considering the independence of such a tribunal, they would look at how the judges were appointed, their term of office and whether they were subject to any pressures which might influence them. The UK system of courts martial was accordingly found not to be convention compliant.

In the Scottish case of *Starrs v The Procurator Fiscal, Linlithgow* (1999), it was held that the system of appointing temporary sheriffs breached the convention. They had no security of tenure and their appointments were subject to annual renewal by the Lord Advocate, a member of the Government.

In *McGonnell v UK* (ECHR, 2000), the role of the Deputy Bailiff of Guernsey, which combined executive and judicial functions, was such as to cast doubt on his independence when dealing with a planning matter. The question whether the Secretary of State for the Environment, Transport and the Regions had the requisite independence when dealing with certain planning matters was considered by the House of Lords in the Alconbury Case (*R. v Environment Secretary Ex p. Holdings and Barnes* (2001)). It was argued that, as the Secretary of State laid down planning policy and issued guidance and framework directions which local authorities and the Planning Inspectorate must follow, he could not act as an independent judge when dealing with disputes. However, the House of Lords advised that there was no violation of Art.6 as any decision by the Secretary of State was appropriately subject to judicial review.

In *R. v Home Secretary Ex p. Anderson and Taylor* (HL, 2002), the House of Lords declared that s.29 of the Crime (Sentences) Act 1997, which allowed the Home Secretary to fix the tariff element of a mandatory life sentence, was incompatible with Art.6.

Figure 8.2: Procedural Impropriety

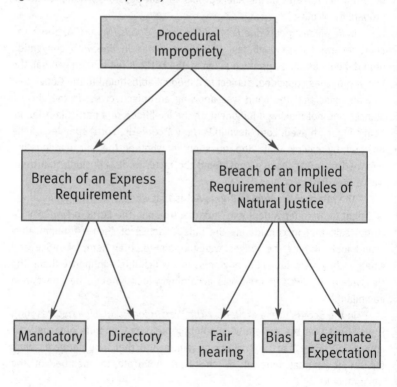

SUMMARY

Having outlined the grounds of judicial review in some detail, it is worth emphasising again the considerable overlap which will occur between the grounds of review outlined. So for example:

> "[t]he exercise of a power for an improper purpose may involve taking irrelevant considerations into account, or ignoring relevant considerations; and either may lead to an irrational result. The failure to grant a person affected by a decision a hearing, in breach of principles of procedural fairness, may result in a failure to take into account relevant considerations" (*Boddington v British Transport Police* (HL, 1998)).

Revision checklist

You should now know and understand:

- the various ground for challenging the legality of decisions made by bodies exercising public law functions, including illegality, irrationality and procedural impropriety;

- the ambiguity surrounding the classification of the different grounds of review;

- the impact of the HRA on the grounds of judicial review.

QUESTION AND ANSWER

The Question

Under the University Discipline Act 2009, the Senate of the University of Oldcastle (a statutory body), has the power to suspend any student, who, in its opinion, is guilty of conduct prejudicial to the good name of the University. Michael, a final year student, has been informed that a sub-committee has taken the decision to expel him following the publication of a series of articles written by him which contain allegations that staff are incompetent, fail to return student work and waste money on expensive trips to foreign conferences. The meeting, which decided to expel Michael, was chaired by Professor Higgins who was singled out for particular criticism in the articles and who has written an angry response published in the press calling for Michael's expulsion.

Consider what action, if any, Michael might take.

Answer Guide

This question is concerned with the grounds of judicial review, particularly whether the student can identify the grounds for review raised in this scenario. The student may begin by identifying the University as a body amenable to judicial review and Michael as an individual with a sufficient interest in the matters raised (see Ch.7)

(1) The **University Discipline Act 2009** gives the Senate the power to suspend a student for conduct prejudicial to the good name of the University. By expelling Michael, it could be argued that the University has acted outside the powers given to it by statute and the decision is therefore ultra vires or illegal (*Att-Gen v Fulham Corp* (HC, 1921)).

(2) As the decision to expel Michael was taken by a sub-committee rather than by the Senate as required by the statute, it may be argued that the body is acting ultra-vires, see *Allingham v The Minister of Agriculture and Fisheries* (HC, 1948). However, there may be an implied power to delegate the power contained in statute. In deciding whether there is an implied power to delegate, the nature of the power and the character of the person will be considered (*Vine v The National Dock Labour Board* (HL, 1957)).

(3) Michael was informed that the decision to expel him had been taken after the fact. It is arguable that Michael's right to a fair hearing have been infringed for a number of reasons, including the failure to inform him of the charges against him (*Kanda v Government of Malaya* (PC, 1962)), and the failure to provide him with the opportunity to present his case (*Local Government Board v Arlidge* (HL, 1915)).

(4) The meeting, which decided to expel Michael, was chaired by Professor Higgins who was singled out for particular criticism in the articles and who has written an angry response published in the press calling for Michael's expulsion. This suggests that there may be some implied procedural impropriety as Michael

has a right to be heard by an unbiased judge (common law and under Art.6(1) of the ECHR), "the question is whether the fair minded and informed observer, having considered the facts, would conclude that there was a real danger of bias." (*Porter v McGill* (HL, 2001)). This may also be evidence of making a decision for an improper purpose or taking irrelevant considerations into account falling foul of the ground of illegality (*Padfield v Minister of Agriculture, Fisheries and Food* (HL, 1968)).

The student should also briefly identify the remedies which may be sought in this case by Michael, namely a quashing order.

Handy Hints and Useful Websites

9

HANDY HINTS

This book is intended to serve as a revision guide, highlighting the key issues in Constitutional and Administrative Law. Accordingly, it should assist as an introduction to the subject, or a summary checklist. Each chapter contains bullet point checklists at the end. These highlight the key issues covered in the chapter (the list at the beginning of each chapter obviously indicates the content to be covered). If you do not understand the revision checklist, reread the relevant section and/or refer to another text for a different presentation of the topic.

The following hints are designed for those preparing for summative assessments in Constitutional and Administrative Law.

1) Read the question carefully

Above all, the key to success in Constitutional and Administrative Law exams is the same as for other exams: read the question carefully to determine what you are being asked before you attempt an answer. A significant number of students write good exam and coursework answers every year but receive low marks because the answer (while possibly accurate) does not address the question set.

2) Practice answers to previous questions

This book provides a number of questions and answers. These can help you learn the skill of answering exam (and coursework) questions. However, generally each university or college will have available a selection of previous exam papers. Moreover, there may be sample coursework questions or, depending on your mode of study, seminar questions, self-test questions or discussion fora questions. These can provide a clear indication of the format of questions you may face. If you are offered the opportunity to submit sample answers in advance of the exam, it is wise to do so. The feedback you will receive will be from the staff who may be marking your assessment. Furthermore, the feedback will help you improve your exam technique, and develop your knowledge before the summative assessment.

3) If in doubt, ask

If you are struggling with an area of law, check with your tutors in advance. They will usually be happy to help diligent students. In addition, there are a plethora of books on the subject, available in most law libraries, bookshops etc. Some are even available online. Although you may have a recommended text, if you encounter problems, it can be worthwhile trying a different text. Authors present ideas differently and, as always, there is no single formula to ensure understanding.

4) Keep up-to-date with UK current affairs

As the introduction notes, so much of Public Law is current affairs (indeed, the name "public" suggest this). Excellent examples of many topics covered in this book appear in the UK news every week. This can make revision easy. If you remain up-to-date with current affairs, you will have many interesting and timely examples to draw on in the exam which should considerably increase your marks (if relevant). To keep up to date, the following sources will help (more websites are listed below):

- read newspapers and analysis of politics and current affairs in the UK;
- listen to or watch sessions of Parliament (available on television, the radio or online). If this proves problematic, you can obviously read Hansard reports of parliamentary sessions;
- listen to or watch UK current affairs news programmes. Again, many of these are available online should you be based outside the UK.

Note that, as with all Law subjects, you must retain a balanced point of view. Unsubstantiated arguments are rarely acceptable in law. It is a legal skill to "see" and understand both sides of an argument. You are certainly entitled to your own opinion but you must be able to justify it drawing on statutes, cases, contemporary examples, etc. A polemical "rant" does not usually demonstrate your understanding of the topic.

5) Enjoy the subject.

Many students find textbook Constitutional and Administrative Law dry. It is, however, a fascinating subject which affects every one of us every day. By finding examples of specific interest to you (e.g. through contacting your local MP, by finding a select committee report of relevance, through voting etc), you are applying your knowledge of the theory and practice of Constitutional and Administrative Law. There are a disproportionate (to some other core subjects) number of sources on Constitutional and Administrative Law and it never fails to be a topical subject. The hard work to learn the basics pays dividend for anyone studying, working or living in the UK.

USEFUL WEBSITES

Official Information

www.parliament.uk—very user-friendly.

www.direct.gov.uk—portal for government information.

www.opsi.gov.uk—Office of Public Sector Information with full text of statutes and statutory instruments available.

www.dca.gov.uk—Department for Constitutional Affairs.

www.dca.gov.uk/peoples-rights/human-rights/index.htm—Human Rights Act Unit at the Department for Constitutional Affairs.

www.homeoffice.gov.uk/police/powers/pace-codes/—up-to-date versions of the **Police and Criminal Evidence Act 1984** (PACE) Codes of Practice.

www.acpo.police.uk—Association of Chief Police Officers of England, Wales and Northern Ireland.

www.ico.gov.uk—the Information Commissioner's Office website.

www.nationalarchives.gov.uk—National Archives, with searchable database of documents, files, etc in the public domain.

www.ombudsman.org.uk—Parliamentary Commissioner for Administration (or Parliamentary Ombudsman).

www.scottish.parliament.uk—Scottish Parliament.

www.scotland.gov.uk—Scottish Executive, with access to a variety of material (reports, laws, etc).

www.assemblywales.org—National Assembly for Wales, with access to a variety of material.

www.niassembly.gov.uk—Northern Ireland Assembly, with access to a variety of material.

www.coe.int—Council of Europe.

http://europa.eu—European Union portal.

www.bbc.co.uk/news—new reports and events, including UK politics.

Courts and Cases

www.supremecourt.gov.uk/current-cases/index.html—for cases currently before the Supreme Court.

www.supremecourt.gov.uk/decided-cases/index.html—for cases decided by the Supreme Court.

www.echr.coe.int—European Court of Human Rights.

www.privy-council.org.uk/output/page1.asp—Privy Council Judgments.

www.bailii.org/databases.html—*Bailii* resource. Very comprehensive and up-to-date.

http://eur-lex.europa.eu/en/index.htm—access to European Union law, including case-law.

Index

This index has been prepared using Sweet and Maxwell's Legal Taxonomy. Main index entries conform to keywords provided by the Legal Taxonomy except where references to specific documents or non-standard terms (denoted by quotation marks) have been included. These keywords provide a means of identifying similar concepts in other Sweet & Maxwell publications and online services to which keywords from the Legal Taxonomy have been applied. Readers may find some minor differences between terms used in the text and those which appear in the index.

(all references are to page numbers)